Henry Ward Beecher, T. J. Ellinwood

A Book of Prayer

From the Public Ministrations of Henry Ward Beecher

Henry Ward Beecher, T. J. Ellinwood

A Book of Prayer

From the Public Ministrations of Henry Ward Beecher

ISBN/EAN: 9783337145071

Printed in Europe, USA, Canada, Australia, Japan

Cover: Foto ©Lupo / pixelio.de

More available books at **www.hansebooks.com**

A Book of Prayer

FROM

THE PUBLIC MINISTRATIONS OF

HENRY WARD BEECHER

COMPILED FROM UNPUBLISHED REPORTS BY

T. J. ELLINWOOD

FOR THIRTY YEARS MR. BEECHER'S SPECIAL STENOGRAPHER

NEW YORK
FORDS, HOWARD, & HULBERT
1892

PREFACE.

THIS little volume is issued in response to repeated solicitations, and in the hope and belief that it will meet with a warm reception and carry peace and consolation to many hearts.

The Introduction is made up of extracts from Sermons and Lecture-room Talks by Mr. Beecher on the subject of Prayer.

The Prayers are selections from unpublished short-hand notes taken at the various weekly services in Plymouth Church, between the years 1858 and 1887. Where practicable, the dates are given; but there are many, originally written out (but not used) for publication with dated sermons, for which the clue of time has been lost. There has been therefore no attempt to arrange them chronologically.

Of course, in the reports of regularly recurring public ministrations one will necessarily come upon many iterations of what might almost be called functional petitions,—such as those for the President of these United States and others joined with him in authority; the Congress; rulers; magistrates, etc., which are proper and necessary in their place and time of delivery, yet not especially edifying in a collection of prayers. Those, therefore, and other similar matter, have been omitted.

In the editing and arrangement of these Prayers I have had the assistance of Mr. John R. Howard, who for so many years enjoyed the confidence of Mr. Beecher in preparing reports of his sermons and other literary matter for issuance in book form.

T. J. E.

BROOKLYN, March, 1892.

TABLE OF CONTENTS.

                                        PAGE

PREFACE, ... 3
INTRODUCTION, ... 7

Prayers:

INVOCATION—PRAYER BEFORE SERMON—CLOSING PRAYER.

Vision of God, ... 21
God in Christ, ... 29
God's Goodness, ... 37
Man's Weakness, ... 43
Filial Courage, ... 48
Parental Responsibility, ... 54
A Sabbath Day, ... 61
For Spiritual Discernment, ... 68
Comfort in Prayer, ... 76
The Wonders of Grace, ... 83
The Sympathy of God, ... 89
At the Close of a Year, ... 95
God's Presence, ... 101
The Greater Life, ... 105
God's Fatherliness, ... 109

	PAGE
The Dullness of Earthly Vision,	114
Refuge from Trouble,	121
Divine Strength for Human Weakness,	126
For Faith in the Unseen,	131
Under Chastisement,	137
The Stability of Faith,	142
The Lesson of Rest,	148
Lowliness and Royalty,	154
Vitality of Goodness,	160
The Better Land,	167
From Generation to Generation,	173
The Communion of Saints,	178
For the Restoration of Faith,	185
The Faithfulness of Christ,	191
For Uplifting,	198
The Privileges of Prayer,	204

INTRODUCTION.

THE NATURE OF PRAYER.

IN its simplest enunciation, prayer is some act by which a human mind comes into communion with God. Its essential nature is the offering to God of our thoughts and feelings. It may be defined as the act of bringing the whole of a man's mind into direct, conscious intercourse with the Divine Mind. It is the coming of a soul into the presence of God for the purpose of communicating to him, as to a parent, its joy, its sorrow, its hope, its fear, its desire, or whatever other experience it may have. It is sunning some thought or feeling in the light of God's face. It is a recognition of God's presence. It is the habit of moving one's thoughts toward God. It is making everything one does, under all circumstances, suggest God, and carry the mind easily where he is. It is as comprehensive in its scope and as varied in its details as all our faculties and their myriad combinations.

No other one exercise of religious feeling has been so universal to the human race. It is not peculiar to Jews and Christians. It is employed alike by men of the true faith and by men of other religions. The idea that the human mind may have commerce with the divinities or with the Deity has been uniformly recognized in all ages, by all nations, and under all conditions of intelligence and civilization. Though the details of prayer, its philosophy, its times and methods, and its possible benefits have been subjects of endless doubt and debate, yet the fact itself that a human being may commune with the Divine Father has been universally accepted.

The tendency to pray is original. It is innate. Provision for it is made in the structure of the mind. However much nations have differed in their customs and religions, the ripest and best natures have tended toward commerce with invisible superior beings, or with the Supreme.

PHASES OF PRAYER.

CLASSIFIED under a few simple heads: prayer may be only an act of confession, and occupy itself in a penitential rehearsal of one's sins and failings. There are moods and seasons in which this should be the burden of every Christian man's prayer, and there are some natures to whom this kind of prayer is more natural than any other.

Or, prayer may be an act of supplication; as when it occupies itself with solicitation for mercies or with deprecation of evils, beseeching the sending down of Divine mercy or the averting of Divine displeasure. This kind of prayer is very comprehensive. It stretches out with endless variation of detail. At times it is suitable for every one; but there are some natures that deal in it too exclusively, their experience in addressing God being almost wholly that of entreaty.

Or, prayer may be a more tranquil exercise of simple communion, in which a loving nature spreads before God the simple life of the hour, as children at evening converse with their parents, or as the disciples under the olive-trees over against Jerusalem related to the Master the events of the day, and received instruction from his lips.

Or, prayer may be an act of thanksgiving, a recognition of God's goodness, an expression of gratitude for blessings received.

Or, finally, prayer may be the simple utterance of praise; as when the soul is made vividly to perceive the wisdom, the beneficence, or the glory of God, in providence or in grace, toward others or toward one's self, in respect to the past, the present, or the future.

While prayer may consist of any or all of these elements, ordinarily they mingle with or succeed each other, the soul ranging from one feeling to another. Each step prepares for the next. The confession of sin introduces a thought of benignity. That enkindles gratitude; and often we come almost unconsciously from an acknowledgment of our unworthiness to the act of praising God. The expression of thanks calls up ideas of Divine goodness and glory, so that the soul cannot but experience admiration. When this is softened by veneration it is simple worship; when it is also enriched by love it is adoration. In any comprehensive Christian experience that utters itself in prayer, confession, supplication, communion, thanksgiving, and praise come and go and blend to form the great whole, as do the tones of different instruments in a well-chorded orchestra. In other words, prayer is the simple interchange of thought and feeling with God; rising out of conscious sensuousness into spirituality; turning one's self away from the things of time, and standing upon the threshold of the eternal world.

Prayer should be just what one feels, just what one thinks, just what one needs; and it should stop the moment it ceases to be the real expression of the need, the thought, and the feeling. It should grow out of an atmosphere of daily experience, and should recognize the whole round of one's life. This is the highest form. And such prayer is easy. Men would pray more and better if they felt that they had a right to pray always, and about everything—as they have. And let it be remembered that aspiration is prayer, that ejaculation is prayer, and that interjection is prayer. Prayers are words in the sentence of the day, and the smallest one is a word. As we grow older we make fewer petitions, though we pray more; and our petitions as we grow older are less and less for ourselves and more and more for our fellow men.

Prayer is not without the intellectual element, but it is essentially a thing of the heart. It springs from a sense of weakness and want, and from a certain spiritual aspiration. It is as certain that the heart lifts itself up to something above it as that sparks and flames lift themselves up into the air when they are kindled. The finer, the larger, the richer, the truer the natures of men are, the more a tendency toward something higher than the mere senses is shown in them. In general, the truest spirit of prayer is that which the most nearly resembles the affectionate, confiding disposition of a little child.

A true praying spirit is one which holds itself in such relations to God that the mood which is predominant is constantly being opened and emptied before him. And if men had liberty, if they felt that prayer was not compulsory, but that it was a conversation, as it were, confined to no prescribed line of subjects, they would find praying a much more profitable exercise than they often do.

UNCEASING PRAYER.

The injunction, "Pray without ceasing," means, not that we are literally to iterate and reiterate the words of prayer, but that we are to give to the praying tendency of the mind that education which we give to faith, to kindness, to conscientiousness and to understanding, and which causes these elements to act continually. We are to make it a tendency—not occasional, but uniform and constant, so that when we are not praying by direct volition there will be a latent aspiration in that direction felt throughout the soul. There is to be such a leaning toward converse with God that every day, every hour, there shall be a movement of the soul toward prayer. The ideal for education in the habit of prayer is the bringing of the soul into a state such that it shall tend perpetually toward communion with God. Not that all other modes of praying are wrong, but that whatever mode is taken should point toward this ideal.

Special occasions of prayer are not to be condemned. There is great benefit in them, even if they are imperfect and if they do less for men than men need to have done. Not only are they not inconsistent with prayer without ceasing, but they may conduce to it. If a man prays on the Sabbath, if he prays in the household, if he has anniversaries of prayer that stand out from his habit of praying in his own thoughts from day to day, he may be said to pray always. He will be like a tranquil lake with islands in it; there will be in his life the uniform praying spirit; and here and there over the surface will be these memorial occasions.

THE LORD'S PRAYER.

THIS universal petition is important as considered in its relations to the framing of theological doctrines. The work of theology is a legitimate work, and this prayer stands, so to speak, as a guide-board to point men to the heavenly Jerusalem, which theologians should heed, and from which they should understand that they cannot take one step toward painting God until they have recognized his fatherhood. Every other divine attribute is to be made subordinate to this. Every man in the world has access to God through this prayer. No matter how sinful he may be, no matter how far he may have wandered from the path of rectitude, there is mercy for every human being that needs mercy and will seek it. The fatherhood of God covers the whole range of our wants. The shortest distance between the world and the Throne above is that between the lip of the penitent and the ear of God; and the moment a man that is sinful has a sense of his sinfulness, and wants God to help him toward righteousness, that moment he has a right to say, "Our Father who art in heaven." He that can utter these words in the fullness of their meaning, or with any considerable appreciation of them, is not far from the kingdom of heaven, from the sonship of God, or from being an heir with Christ to all the glory of an eternal inheritance.

LIBERTY OF PRAYER.

IT is the right, even of those who are not possessed of strong feelings of any kind, to pray. Prayer, being the offering of one's thoughts and feelings to God, should always have a relation to the nature that employs it. There is such a thing as growth in prayer; but the first quality of Christian liberty is the right of every man to lisp if he cannot speak; to speak in broken numbers if he is not fluent; to pray in small circuits if he cannot in large. Each one is to bring to his Father just that mind which has been given to him. As it is in the habit of expression among ourselves, so it may be and so it should be in the habit of expressing ourselves in communion with God. Great simplicity, the utmost frugality of expression, in prayer, satisfies some natures, and they have a right to it; nor should they chafe and fret in their conscience as if they were delinquent because they cannot pray as eloquent men of tumultuous expression do. Eloquence is a beautiful and useful gift, but it is not indispensable to prayer. This liberty ought not to be so construed as to prevent growth and enriching; but, as an initial experience, simplicity of devotion is genuine. The presentation of thoughts and feelings consciously to God is prayer; the presentation to God of the thoughts and feelings of one who is without veneration—if his unvenerating nature be conscientious—is prayer; and the presentation to God of the thoughts and feelings of one whose predominant sentiment is love is prayer; but the prayer of each is partial. He that prays only by veneration, or by conscience, or by affection, is a partialist. He is like a musician that has no scale, and plays on a monochord. Every man should seek to add to the richness of his gifts by mingling others with them.

DANGERS OF PRAYER.

ONE of these is the superstitious, unintelligent idea that there is something in praying which will produce blessings without regard to whether or not it is an utterance of the thoughts and feelings of the heart. The more intelligent one's prayer is, the better he understands it and the more consciously he brings his thoughts and feelings into the presence of God,—the more he will be blessed.

The next danger of prayer is that of formality, which leads to poverty, narrowness, meagerness. Men fall into habits of formality in both extemporaneous and written prayers; and formalities invariably diminish the profit of prayer, simply because in their use one set of expressions is made to perform the service of all sorts of feelings.

Another danger is that of selfishness in prayer. It besets particularly Christians that are advanced in religious life, and to whom prayer has become a constant or at least a frequent exercise. This danger is one that especially belongs to intense natures; but all natures are more or less subject to it. We should be in such sympathy with God that we should have much to pray for as touching the honor and glory of his name; we should be in such sympathy with divine Providence that we should have much to offer thanksgiving for, in the events that every day transpire around about us; and we should be in such sympathy with our fellow-men that we should find in their wants much subject-matter for petition.

NATURALNESS OF PRAYER.

Do you hesitate about praying, on the ground that you do not know how? Prayer is very simple to one who has a correct conception of it. There are few persons who cannot say, "God, I thank thee for the morning." If you have gone so far, and cannot go any further, you have prayed. When you step out of doors you have prayed if you say, "God, I thank thee for this bright day." Cannot you say, "I thank God for the sunlight"? You may not know how to pray as Deacon A. does; but do you not know how to pray as the poor sinner does? Think what is the mercy that stands next to you, and thank God for that. If a servant brings you anything, you say, "Thank you"; if you are well-bred, you say "Thank you" when your companion does you a service; you never look upon any token of a person's kindness to you that your feelings do not move in gratitude toward that person: and can you live in God's world, where every minute is loaded with his thoughtfulness of you, and not say, "I thank you"? To look at a flower, and say, "I thank God for that"; to look at the sky, and say, "Through it my thoughts rise toward God;" to look at one's friends, and say, "God be thanked for them"; to think of their love, forgiveness, forbearance and helpfulness, and say, "I thank God for these"—this is praying.

There ought to be such gladness, such delight, in praying, that when we go to God it shall be heart-hunger that takes us to him. As he created us, and made the chords of joy—yes, even of mirth—in us, and as communion with him is bringing the whole soul to him, we have a right to prayer in that direction. The heart may feel an inspiration and a rapture in the presence of God which it cannot experience anywhere else. If God gave you a tendency to rise in rapturous prayer, it is your liberty to employ that element in your communion with him. If we will but cultivate in God's direction the natural tendencies with which each one of us is furnished, we have the privilege of all joy and happiness in our intercourse with our heart's Father.

How fruitful is prayer the moment you take it out of the ecclesiastical routine! How natural; how helpful; how satisfactory!

A BOOK OF PRAYER.

Invocation.

OUR Father, we come not as those that are empty; for we are full of hope. Thy love, and the mercies that drop down from thee—thy tender mercies and thy loving kindness—they wrap us around as with a robe. We walk as enclosed by the very heart of God; and night and day, wherever we are, we are with thee. We are heirs of all things, because the Lord is ours. When we ask for ourselves, it is not as if we needed, or as if thou didst need to be persuaded: it is in love. We desire to ask what we need; thou hast made it sweet as well as needful. And now, vouchsafe to us the disclosures of thyself this day. May we know thy presence. As the sea knows when storms are gone and the sun shines, so may we in our tranquillity know that God is present with us. Set us free from doubt, from burden, from fear, and from all worldliness; and grant that we may find in the exaltation of our affections, in our fellowship one with another, and in our fervor of devotion that thou art present. So may the services of the morning and of the day, here, at our homes and everywhere, be blessed of God, through Jesus Christ, our Lord.

Vision of God.

Sunday Morning, May 6, 1877.*

WE rejoice, O Lord our God, not in ourselves nor in the firm earth on which we tread, nor in the household, nor in the church, nor in all the procession of things where mankind moves with power and glory. We rejoice in the Lord. We rejoice in thy strength. A strange joy it is. Day by day we find ourselves breaking out into gladness through the ministration of the senses, and by the play of inward thought; but thou art never beheld by us. We may never lay our hand upon thine, nor look into thy face, as did thy disciples of old. Thou never speakest to us, nor do we feel thy hand, nor do we discern thy face of love and glory and power. We break away from all other experiences, and look up into the emptiness, as it seems to us, which yet is full of life; into that which seems cold and void, but wherein moves

* Immediately following the reception of members into the church.

eternal power; into the voiceless and inscrutable realm where thou dwellest, God over all, blessed forever. Our thoughts have been taught to go there, and our eye has been taught to discern and to rejoice in the invisible, with all the strength of our nature, as if before us was the Celestial City; we shout again in songs of praise; and in the silence of thought we cry out to those that live there in holy companies. They are to us as if they were in our midst. There is no winter in our sky. There is no death above our head. There are no sorrows there that beat remorselessly as the sea upon the shore. There are no tears there. There is no change there except from glory to glory. Eternal rest moves with eternal activity.

O Lord our God, how near thou art to us! and we do not know it. How near is the other life! and we do not feel it. It clothes us as with a garment. It feeds us. It shines down upon us. It rejoices over us. Now and then we catch the inspiration, and some feeble joy uprises. Some sympathy interprets to us what is going on beyond the bound of the city. We glory in the Lord, and in his kingdom, and in the great invisible realm where royalties belong to us, where our crowns are waiting, and where our rest remains—the rest that remaineth for the people of God. Thither, out of narrow and anguishful ways, out of sorrows, out of regrets, out of bereavements, we look; and already we are rested before we reach it. Leaving out the things of time, we walk emancipated and glorified.

Grant unto us, to-day, we beseech thee, this beatific vision. ⁕ We need it for the solace of our care. We need it because of the wickedness which overpowers many. We need it because on every side we are hedged in, and are made to feel how small humanity is, on what narrow ways it walks, how easily it is cast down, how weak it is to help itself, how time grinds us, and how we are pushed everywhither toward infirmity. In youth, strength beckons us to embrace it; but after we have reached manhood we wax toward diminishing power—nay, not *toward* it, but *beyond* it, to youth again; to unwasting power; to riches and joys that dwell at thy right hand for evermore.

We pray in behalf of all that are present for such a ministration of the spirit, this morning, as shall make dull things bright, heavy things light, and discouragements cheerful. May they who are thy children know how to bring light out of darkness. May those who walk disguised in the garments of this life behold the white and shining raiment that is theirs. May none feel useless, worthless, on whom the blood of Christ has rested, and on whom immortality shall yet wait. May we lift ourselves up in the midst of despondencies, as beseems the children of the living God.

Draw near to all that are here. Baptize them with the Holy Spirit. Give them the vision and insight of faith. Help them to take hold mightily, by the hands of their souls, upon the fruit of the tree of life, or haply, at least, upon the leaves which shall be for their healing.

We pray that thou wilt be with those who are not with us, and yet are with us in our thoughts, daily. We pray that thou wilt sustain them, if they be upon the sea, if they walk in other lands, or if they roam in distant parts of our own land, fulfilling the errands of thy providence. To-day many thoughts come hither and go out hence. This place is to many as Jerusalem was to thy servants of old; and many pray for us and with us, and we pray for them and with them.

Are any greatly sick? We pray that their sickness may seem to them as a golden gate; and may they long to depart and be with Christ, which is better than life.

We pray that those who are watching and carrying burdens for others may be strengthened by the consciousness that they are doing as the Master did, and that they rule through service.

We pray, O Lord our God, that thou wilt bless all those who are about to unite themselves to this church, before men, in visible relations. Fill them, we beseech of thee, with the power of the Holy Spirit. May none of them stumble, or be discouraged by the greatness of the way. Grant that they may come into our midst as new buds break out in a garden among blossoms and leaves, and that they may bring forth much fruit. We pray for the young among them, that they may be able to discern danger, and resist it; to perceive temptation, and overcome it; and to count themselves good soldiers of the Lord Jesus Christ. Deliver them from snares. Rescue them from the wily and the evil-seeking. Make them strong in the Lord.

And, Father, may others be brought in, a great company, from the world, from selfishness, from self-indulgence, from stumbling vices, from all manner of evil. May their thoughts be turned to the nobler way, to the new life, to the treasure of the invisible, to the royalty which they owe to the Lord their God. May thy kingdom come in this church, and thy will be done here as it is done in heaven.

We pray for those who pray, and for those who pray not. We pray for those who are afflicted;

for those whose backs are turned upon the right way; for those who watch, and for those who forget and slumber.

We beseech of thee, Father almighty, that thou wilt bless, not us alone, but all the assemblies that are gathered to-day to worship in the name of the Lord Jesus Christ. Be with thy servants every one. Strengthen them to do their Master's will in their Master's spirit.

We pray for thy cause throughout this land, and in all lands. We thank thee that we abide now in peace, and that no blood flows in our midst. Remember the nations that are despoiled by war. Make haste, thou Emancipator of mankind! When shall the day come in which fetters shall no longer bind, in which bolt and bar shall no longer imprison, in which cruelty shall no longer domineer, and in which men shall weep less and laugh more! Bring forth, O Lord God, the day of prediction; let thy sun come toward the horizon that brings the morning twilight; and may the light shine brighter and brighter unto the perfect day.

Closing Prayer.

WE are journeying over the rough and thorny ways of life with unsandaled feet. Lord, we need the power of God. We need to be taken up into the arms of thy mercy, and of thy long-suffering love. We need to be carried upon thy bosom, as a mother bears her little children. Lift us up. Give us confidence, that we may believe that there is something more than morals, something more than earthly joy, in following Jesus. Give us a belief in that invisible and spiritual temper of the soul which brings all sadness to an end, and all joy to a consummation.

Invocation.

AMID the thunder of the praise of heaven, amid the rejoicings of infinite love, what are the voices which men can utter, O Lord, our God! Yet, in the midst of all earthly songs of joy or revelry the cry of the child brings quick the father and mother to it; and in thine ear the cry of trouble, the voice of want, the yearning and desire even of silence, are more than the tumultuous praise and rejoicing of victorious life. Thou that art more thoughtful for the one that is in the wilderness than for the ninety-and-nine that are safe, listen to us; for our outcry is of necessity. We need thee, we need thy light, thine interpretation of truth, thy guidance and thy victory. Even so, open thine hand, O Lord Jesus, and say to us, Lo, I am with you: peace be unto you!

God in Christ.

Oct. 18, 1868.

O, THOU who hast slept, thou whom the rock didst embrace and darkness infold—thou art come forth! It is eternal morning with thee. Death is beneath thy feet. From thine hands shine out the rays of eternal life. Infinite bounty is thine. Thou that wert stripped of all things, and rejected; thou whose very raiment was poor—in thine eternal fullness thou art now clothing all, feeding all, governing all. Thou hast been the lowest and the least, the cast out and the despised: thou art exalted at the right hand of God to be a Prince and a Saviour. And thou hast succor for all that are unbefriended; sympathy for all that are alone; suggestion and inspiration for all that are perplexed and blinded. Thy soul comes forth more boldly and widely than the sun itself; and thou art carrying seasons through all thine illimitable universe that have in them no winter, no retrocession; for there is eternal light and eternal warmth, and eternal growth and blessedness, wherever thou art. We have felt thy power. We have been transformed by it. We have felt the old man destroyed or wounded or cast down, and the new man awakened within us. And now we look upon all things with different values. No longer the things which the sense beholds are greatest to us. Nor is the strength of life in the outward kingdom. Therefore, in the invisible is more than in the visible; in things that are unseen more treasures than in things that are seen.

We thank thee that this beginning-work is going on, and that thou, the Author of it, will be the Finisher of it. For we lift up our souls to thee, and pray that we may be wholly subdued to thy spiritual wisdom, and that the might of the outward man—that which we share with the lion and the beast—we may rise above. Thou hast strength of consolation, strength for grander thoughts and nobler purposes. Thou hast the power of love and the power of universal beneficence. Grant that we may have in us the power of truth and equity and justice and love. So may the kingdom of God come into our souls, whilst thou art governing all things by the word of thy power. We thank thee that thou art building within the outward realm the fairer kingdom where meekness and gentleness shall rule; where thy power shall be of the soul and not of the right hand of omnipotence. We aspire to that kingdom. We long to be joined to those that are seeking it. We bless thy name that we are joined to thee; but our footsteps desire to take hold of those nobler and loftier strides, which the apostles and disciples and holy martyrs took. There they are to-day waiting—nay, not waiting, but blessedly active—in thy kingdom. Justified are they, and made perfect—not forgetting their worldly experience, yet elevated far above it. We aspire to their society. We are of them. Our souls know their relationship. There is that in us which calls for them. We rejoice that our hearts go out to all that yet live around about us; but we do not forget those that are gone before. They are our companions not less because we linger in imperfection and they have taken hold upon perfect blessedness. Our hearts go out for all that have been like thee—for that great and glorious train of obscure ones who in prisons, in dungeons, or in the wilderness, have been sawn asunder, or stoned, or burned, and slain in a thousand cruel ways, and have reached through suffering the peace and blessedness of thy heavenly kingdom. They, too, are our brethren of this fellowship. We are reaching forward toward it, and in our way contesting things within and things without. Thou art every day inspiring us to it. To this conflict we are girded by thine own invisible hand. Our hearts feel thee; our spirits seize thee. Thou art not speaking with men's voices; yet we hear thee speaking to us, and every day are encouraged to make new battle, to gird up our loins again, to put on the whole armor of God; and having done all things, to stand.

And now, O Lord, how shall we thank thee for the hope and the joy of the present, and for the infinite promise of the future! How can we thank thee for the reality of this gift—for the glory and the amplitude of it, that we are permitted to love thee, that our love is accepted, that thou hast opened the palace door of thy soul, and that we enter in, and are in thee and of thee! Thou camest to our poverty, thou camest down to our weakness. While we lie level along the ground, troubled and cast down, thou dost find us, forgive us, encourage us, and put us again upon strength to walk along the right way.

How shall we make mention of thy faithfulness with words enough tender and endearing! How shall we praise thee enough! All our memories of thy goodness to us, at times flock upon us. Thy mercies are more than the leaves of the forest. They are more than all the drops of the dew that fall at night upon flowers, and are purer and sweeter, infinitely. Thy goodness has been boundless. We have been walking through it as through the wilderness, seeing but the part—unable to see the whole. Thou hast passed across our souls with influences. Oh, if we had known them, and their meaning, what music and gladness wouldst thou have awakened within us! But too often we have been as strings unstrung; and while the Master was there, we had no music. Yet we thank thee for thy meaning; and for so much as has been gained upon our faithlessness and backwardness and lowness. We confess our imbecility and pride and selfishness. We confess how we are weighed down, and how evermore we are gravitating and sinking toward the earth. Yet, by thine inspiration, we thank thee that there has been that informing spirit and upward tendency, and that we have not been carried back again to the very soil on which we tread. How shall we thank thee for all those sweet links of sympathy and hope by which we are made so much to each other! We thank thee for all our homes. We thank thee for all our loves and affections. We thank thee for our aspirations, and for all that blessedness of interlinked love by which we are feebly and imperfectly practising here those paces which we shall interpret in a nobler way when we come to walk in the heavenly kingdom, and among perfected society.

We pray now, O Lord, that thou wilt still be merciful and faithful to us. We do not love thy darkness; yet come in night, if need be, to wake us from slumber. We do not like thy rod, yet smite us therewith, if there be mercy in thy heart. We do not like to be overturned, and to have our way set back, yet thy will be done, and not ours!

Grant, we beseech of thee, thou Lover, the work of love, which desires perfectness. Secure it in us, though it cost tears and sighs and suffering. May we know the suffering Saviour, and be willing to be suffering disciples. May we not seek pain nor turn aside from it. May we not seek mortification nor be unwilling to bear it. May we seek only the things that are of Christ, in ourselves and in others, and take whatever Providence sends, patiently, quietly, expectantly, and confidently.

We beseech of thee, O Lord, thy blessing to rest on all whom we love. Sanctify all our friendships, ennoble them, and give them something of that atmosphere which we hope they shall have—substantial immortality. Bless, we pray thee, all our families; our children; our brothers and sisters; our dear absent ones. Remember those that are upon the sea, and those that are in far-off lands. Remember the lost and the wandering, and bring them back. Remember all that are our enemies. Set us free from animosity toward all men. Make us forgiving, and give a better mind to those that hate us. Teach us how to live for the best things and the noblest, bearing one another's burdens, being patient with one another's mistakes, and seeking by love to repair the mischiefs that selfishness is working in this world, until thy labor is consummated, and our turn shall have come.

Then forth from thine eternity shall fly the swift voice of angels to call us home; and then may men rejoice more than when one is born into life, that another is set free.

Closing Prayer.

ACCEPT our thanks, O Father, for the radiancy of the truth as made known to us in Jesus Christ, our Lord. Forbid that we should disfigure the brightness of thy glory, the face of thy love, by fears and by doubts. Give to thy people, in their own experience, those elements by which they can interpret God to mankind, so that they shall be drawn by goodness—not driven by fear; coming as lovers come—not scourged and afraid. Give to us such thoughts of thee and such comfort in thee that our own experience shall be full of sweetness, solicitation and encouragement to those around about us.

Bless all present, to-day. May they go God-laden to their homes. And grant, we pray thee, that as they who walk in a garden have the perfume with them even to their garments, so we may, from the sanctuary, more delightful than frankincense and myrrh, bear the sweet fragrance of the love of God with us.

Invocation.

BE pleased, our Father, not only to be present by that general power with which the world is filled, but to grant unto us that special influence from thy Spirit that shall awake in us some affection, some faith, some hope, that there may be the dawn of the soul, and that we may rejoice, as outwardly in the rising of the sun, so inwardly in the rising of the Sun of Righteousness with healing in his beams. We pray that we may have help to speak from thy Word, to consider its truths, and to draw from them the nourishment of our lives. Bless us in our communion with thee, inspire us with right desires, and teach us how to pray.

God's Goodness.

Sunday Morning, May 20, 1877.

WE thank thee, our Father, that thou hast made the way of prayer to be a way of pleasantness and of peace. Thou hast taken the lions out of the way, thou hast stopped the caves of despair, and all the pits are filled which fear hath dug. A way is cast up, and the ransomed of the Lord return thereon with songs and joy on their heads.

We have traversed that way; and though it is sometimes strait and narrow, we have found it a way of strength.

Grant unto us the evidence in our souls that thou hearest prayer. We pray that thou wilt give us that rest, that peace, which passeth all understanding. Grant, we pray thee, that in the hours of solitude we may find thee companionable. In times of despondency hear us, thou Morning Star, and bring on the day. In times of sorrow and of affliction may our voice be to thee as the child's voice in the night is to the mother, that brings her to it; and in every time of need may we come boldly to the throne of grace to obtain mercy and help.

We rejoice to believe that with thee it is more blessed to give than to receive, and that our petitions are pleasant to thee. Thou art not weary. Thou dost not give that thou mayest rid thyself of importunity: thou givest out of the abundance of thine own heart. Thou grantest unto us the things which we need. Thou dost for us exceedingly above what we ask or think, for thine own name's sake.

We rejoice that we dwell with no narrow, stern judge, who loves law more than those who are under it. Thou art our Father and our Mother.

GOD'S GOODNESS.

All that which is best and deepest in the hearts of those who love us on earth, is as a speck, compared with the infinite Sun of Righteousness. All thy soul moves with currents infinite and fathomless, and all thy purposes are for ultimate kindness, and for the final good of thy creatures. We draw near to thy bountifulness, and rejoice in thee. We rejoice though we are imperfect; though we are sinful; though we are not faithful to our word, nor to our knowledge; though we often go back upon friendship, and upon honor, and upon truth, with thee, the Dearest and Best, as if thou wert the worst. We rejoice that in the fullness and greatness of thy nature we have peace, and rest, and hope, and inspiration, and are to have final salvation. This is a gift, through Jesus our Lord. We take it by faith. We inherit it. It is the gift of God, without equivalent and without condition. Out of the fullness and grandeur of thine own nature thou art pouring forth treasures upon us.

And now, O Lord, we desire to walk in the faithfulness of love and of holy trust. And in the time to come we desire not to let anything daunt us. For when have we been forsaken of Thee? When the waters rose, and when the fires were fierce, thou didst rescue us from the deep, and save us from the flames. And thou hast saved our souls from the lions. Thou hast saved us from those that would hurt and destroy us. Where, in poverty, has there been an enemy that thou hast not destroyed? Where, in bereavements, has there been a poisoned edge that thou hast not turned away from our hearts? Where, in solitariness, in weakness, in despondency, in soul-hunger, in unrest of heart, has there been the place that thou hast not been with us, to commune and to graciously console?

Thou God of the inward life as well as of all creation, we beseech of thee that the time past may suffice for doubt, for fear, and for distress, and that in the time to come we may trust thee implicitly, and rest upon thee, sure that thou wilt carry our souls over the gulf, and through the darkness, because thou art God, and art unchangeable, the same yesterday, to-day, and forever.

Manifest thyself, thou who art our God and our souls' Saviour, to all who are in thy presence, and to each as he severally needs. Call every one by name, that he may know that God knows him. Be the God, not of mankind alone, but of every one of us, this day. Accept the services of song which we offer thee. Accept our desires for instruction, that we may be better than we are, and fulfill the duties of life better than we have done.

Breathe, we beseech of thee, upon us the dew of heaven, in the relations which we sustain to each other in the midst of human affairs.

O Lord, we pray that thou wilt grant grace to all, so that as their day is their strength may be also. Remember the aged, and prepare them for the glory which lies but just before them. Remember those who are in the battle of life. Grant that they may gird up their loins, having on the whole armor of God. And having done all things, may they be able still to stand.

We pray for those who are coming into life, that they may come with hope and self-confidence not only, but with the faith of God. May they have the shield of faith by which to quench the fiery darts of temptation. May they be delivered from every snare. May they enter upon Christian manhood with more nobility and purity of character than we have evinced. As they rise into life wilt thou more perfectly equip them in the Christian spirit.

We pray for our land; and not only for our own nation, but for those on our border, that they may thrive and prosper. We pray for all the nations of the earth. Wilt thou not quench the brand of war? Wilt thou not at last furl the banner of darkness and death? O Dove, bring forth the white banner, and let it be outrolled, and spread. And let the trumpet cease to sound; let the sword be forgotten; let cruelty return to the pit; and let the whole earth rejoice in thy salvation.

Closing Prayer.

ACCEPT our thanks, Almighty God, for all the mercies in thy revelation, and for the augmentation of that life which makes the revelation of divine truth in thy Word clearer and clearer by the experience of outward life. Cleanse us from mistake, from superstition, and from ignorance. Give us believing, trusting hearts, not for fear, but for love's sake. May that ladder which Jacob saw with his head upon the stone be given also to those who have been taught to lie upon the ground with but a stone for their pillow. May the angels of God be seen ascending and descending; and though the bottom of the ladder be upon the ground, may the top be in heaven. So bless us, we beseech of thee, because thou lovest us; and teach us to love thee, and to live a life of love for Christ's sake.

Invocation.

By thine own Spirit breathe into us that light, O our Father, which shall awaken in us the spirit of children and spiritual sight. May we arouse from sloth, from the slumber of the senses, from all mere worldly things, and come into that realm where thou dwellest, which is peopled with thy thought of love toward us. May we catch the divine inspiration, and by faith discern thee. Grant that we may hold communion to-day with thee, and behold the eternal verities which can be seen only by the spirit, and rejoice in the substance of those hopes which thou hast held out to us through Jesus Christ, our Lord. Accept our service of song. Look with favor upon our devotion and upon our efforts at instruction. Help us to rejoice with each other this day, as though we sat in the very gate of heaven.

Man's Weakness.

Our Father, we do not need to draw near to thee as suppliants, to persuade thee. Thy compassion is over all the works of thine hand. Thy bounty is from eternity to eternity. Thy heart breathes forth goodness and mercy—and this is thy nature. Infinite power, infinite goodness, infinite wisdom—

that is God; we do not need to make it known to thee but ourselves to realize it. We come before thee to-night to confess our unworthiness, and our consciousness of it; to make known to thee our sense of thy goodness to us individually, and to this church; and to give thee thanks. In the days gone by thou hast been more to us than thou hast promised. Thou hast done exceeding above all that we asked or thought; and to thy great name be the praise and the glory. We desire to confess, O Lord, that we have not lived according to our promises, nor according to the thoughts and intents of our hearts. We have felt the gravitation of things that drew us downward from things high and holy. We have followed right things how feebly! Weak are we to resist the attraction of evils that lurk about the way of goodness; and we are conscious that we walk in a vain show. We behold and approve thy law, but find it hard to obey; and our obedience is of the outside, and not of the soul and of the spirit, with heartiness and full of certainty. We rejoice that thou art a Teacher patient with thy scholars, and that thou art a Father patient with thy children. Thou art a God of long-suffering goodness, and of tender mercies, and therefore we are not consumed.

And now we beseech of thee, O thou unwearied

One, that thou wilt inspire us with a heavenly virtue. Lift before us the picture of what we should be and what we should do, and maintain it in the light, that we may not rub it out in forgetfulness; that we may be able to keep before ourselves our high calling in Christ Jesus. And may we press forward, not as they that have attained or apprehended; may we press toward the mark, for the prize of our high calling in Christ Jesus, with new alacrity, with growing confidence, and with more and more blessedness of joy and peace in the soul.

Vouchsafe, we pray thee, to all in thy presence, divine illumination and quickening. Grant that those who are remiss, that those who are slumbering, that those who slide back easily from their own vows and purposes, may be upheld by thy free Spirit. May they be touched in heart and in conscience, and raised to new spiritual life.

Sustain thou, O Lord, all those who are seeking to maintain their fidelity to thee and thy cause under trouble and difficulty. May they be accepted of thee. May they not be vanquished by the powers of the world, but upheld by thy saving Spirit.

We pray for all those who have no knowledge of Christ Jesus, and no personal life in him, that they may be brought to know the Saviour; that they may discern his beauty; that they may believe in his power; that they may trust in his grace. May Christ be formed in their souls more and more.

Wilt thou plentifully endow with divine grace thy servants in the ministry who endeavor to lead men to the Shepherd and Bishop of their souls. Bless all our schools and Bible classes. Bless all those who go forth from this church to minister to the poor, the neglected, and the needy. May the influence which goes forth from this sanctuary be as a light in a dark place to comfort and rebuke and save. May thy cause have free course among us, to run and be glorified. And we pray for all those who seek the amelioration of manners; all who uphold thy law; all who study the welfare of the times. Wilt thou hold in the hollow of thine hand the hearts of our rulers, and lead them in right ways; and, we beseech of thee, watch over this great people. May thy blessing rest evermore upon this land, and upon all the nations of the earth.

And to Thy name shall be the praise, Father, Son, and Spirit. *Amen.*

Closing Prayer.

OUR Father, be pleased to follow with thy blessing the word of truth spoken. Make it powerful upon the understanding, upon the heart, and upon the conscience. Forgive those that are out of the way, and bring them back to the Shepherd and Bishop of their souls. Forgive those that do not forgive us. If we have made any our enemies by our own misconduct, give us repentance therefor. If any hate us without cause, give them repentance and us love. May we bear about with us the spirit of the Lord Jesus Christ so effectually that the light of his attributes shall be manifest in us—the same patience, the same affection, the same fidelity, the same love, the same purity. Guide thy people through the wilderness. Fulfill thy promises to them. May they walk in green pastures and by the side of still waters. And we beseech of thee that when thou hast served thyself with us in this mortal life, thou wilt be pleased, through infinite mercy, to take us to thyself, where sin shall be but a sad memory, and where holiness shall be our joy for evermore.

Invocation.

WE send our voices and our thanksgiving forth to thee, not as to one afar off, to whom our songs become faint from the distance; for thou art a God near unto every one of us. And not alone dost thou hear that which we speak: that which we think sounds in thine ear; and that which we feel and that which lies fallow both of thought and feeling are perfectly well known unto thee. Accept not only our thought and feeling, but all those unmeasured elements from which spring both thought and feeling. And grant to us, to-day, that divine pressure, that moulding power, by which all our inward life is shaped which issues forth in conduct. Consecrate us, and make us sons of God, so that our innermost and spontaneous outcry toward thee shall be, evermore, *Father.* Bless us in reading, in singing, in speaking, in every service of song, at our homes, in our thoughts, in our labor, in all the schools where we may be placed, and make it a day of heaven to us.

Filial Courage.

TWIN MOUNTAIN HOUSE.

O LORD our God, thy greatness is unsearchable, and the glory of thy presence has overwhelmed us. Thou art hidden in excess of light; and if we were to behold thee in the great sphere in which thou art living, none of us would dare to draw near to thee. Our imperfections, our transgressions, our secret thoughts, our wild impulses, that at times come surging in upon us, are such that we should be ashamed to stand before the All-searching Eye. Our lives are before thee, open as a book, and thou readest every word and every letter thereof. Blessed be thy name, thou hast taught us to come to thee through the Lord Jesus Christ as through a friend, and thou hast taught us to draw near to thee in person through the familiar way of Fatherhood; from our childhood we have said, Our Father, and in this way we are not afraid; in this way we come familiarly and boldly: not irreverently, but with the familiarity which love gives. Thou hast poured the light of thy love upon the path which we tread, and thou hast taught us to come rejoicing before thee, and to make confession of our sins, that they may be pardoned, and to draw near to thee, feeling that what is deficient in us is made up by the abundant generosity of thy nature. And so, this morning, united by common infirmities, with common transgressions, with wavering hope, with tremulous fear, with bereavements, with sorrows, with courage and with rejoicing, united in all ways one with another, we desire to come before thee, and to receive a common blessing. Open thy hand and thy heart, and say to every one of us, Peace be unto you!

Accept our thanksgiving for multiplied mercies. Accept our thanksgiving for so much of illumination as we have had. Thou hast dealt with us, we know. We know that something in us yearns for thee. The flowers break forth, they know not why; but we know it is because the sun shines on them. And we know that whatever leads upward in us must be from the shining of the Sun of righteousness. Thou art present, and we are conscious of it. We cannot comprehend the glory and the grandeur of thy power; but our hearts reach up towards purity, towards truth, towards strength and goodness. We long for virtue. We long for cleansing and purified powers of thought and emotion. We long for more harmony in ourselves and in each other. We long for knowledge of that great realm around about us and above us where no earthly foot hath trod, in thy spiritual kingdom.

We beseech of thee, O Lord our God, that thou wilt grant to every one of us in thy presence, this morning, the special mercies which he needs—strength where weakness prevails, and patience where courage has failed. Grant, we pray thee, that those who need long-suffering may find themselves strangely upborne and sustained. Grant that those who wander in doubt and darkness may feel distilling upon their soul the sweet influence of faith. Grant that those who are heart-weary, and sick from hope deferred, may find the God of all salvation. Confirm goodness in those that are seeking it. Restore, we pray thee, those who have wandered from the path of rectitude. Give every one honesty. May all transgressors of thy law return to the Shepherd and Bishop of their souls with confession of sin, and earnest and sincere repentance.

We pray that thy blessing may go forth, not only upon those who are now waiting in thy presence, but upon all whom our thoughts follow. Wherever we love, love thou; and where we would bless, bless thou. Grant, we pray thee, that all those whom we have left behind, that all our dear friends scattered abroad through the wide world, may be united to-day, and may meet us at the feet of our blessed Saviour.

We pray that this family, gathered together casually, by the wayside, may abide in that spirit and in that rejoicing which come from the love of the Lord Jesus Christ. We pray for every one, and for thy kingdom in the heart of every one;

and for the glory of thy holy name as it is manifested in thy children.

We pray for this whole region around about; for the household that belongs here, and that ministers to us in worldly things. We pray for the sick, for the poor, for the ignorant, for the needy, and for the whole world, that the day of clashing arms may cease, that the thunder of battle may be heard no more, that the blessing of righteousness may descend and fall upon the earth, and that there may spring up and come forth abundantly the fruits of righteousness.

O Lord, may the time speedily come when all the earth shall know thy salvation, and when thou shalt reign in the power of love from the rising of the sun until the going down of the same.

Closing Prayer.

Our Father, may the message of truth be blessed to the enlightenment and the comfort of every one. May we learn to respect thy laws, especially the inward laws of God, which belong to us—to our inward life. May we learn what they are, pondering the things in nature, and the things in thy Word. We pray that we may be inspired to more and more care of ourselves. We are royal. We are sons of God. May we remember that soon we go home from our school; and may we be eager to appear with honor before our Father, that waits for us. But grant that we may not, while seeking to make ourselves great and strong and wise and good, forget to be gracious, nor fall into selfishness. Deliver us, on the one and on the other hand, and finally perfect us and bring us home.

Invocation.

BEHOLD us, our Father, as we behold our little children, only with that infinite love and compassion which make thee God. We adore thee, and wonder at thy power and at thy wisdom. Grant, this morning, that there may be rejoicing in our hearts at thy love and sympathy. Draw near, and make known thyself to each one. Come to the sorrowing, to the burdened, to the dark of mind, to the doubting, to all. And may the services of the day fill us with the inspiration of God, and prepare us for all the duties of life.

Parental Responsibility.*

WE thank thee, our Father, for the blessed scenes of this morning. We thank thee for the presence of these little ones among thy servants. We thank thee that thou art opening our hearts in sympathy and love toward them. And we pray for them, together, all of us, that they may be brought up in the nurture and admonition of the Lord, that the sweetness of virtue may be theirs, that they may early come to piety, and that they may be able to

* Immediately following the baptism of children.

PARENTAL RESPONSIBILITY. 55

endure the trials and temptations that lie before them, and prove themselves in manhood worthy to be called sons of God.

We beseech of thee that thy Spirit may rest upon those who are to guide these children, and endue them with wisdom plentifully. May they be to their children examples of that which they teach. So may they bear their sins, their weaknesses and their sicknesses as thou didst bear our sorrow and wert afflicted with our trouble. We pray that as they stand between these young souls and God there may be no misinterpretation of the divine Spirit. May they appear in all gentleness, in all patience, in all forbearance, in all long-suffering, in all purity of thought, of feeling, and of every deed. In all self-denial and burden-bearing may they interpret to their children, through their own lives, the divine nature.

Grant that these children may grow up. And yet, if thou shalt call them home before the summer is over, before they have reached the harvest-field of life, prepare thy servants, that, in the opening of the heavenly gate to receive these little ones, their faith may discern there their portion and their treasure, as they shall weep for their children.

Bless all the children of this congregation, belonging to our several families, and belonging to the several schools, beloved, wherein we are gathering the homeless and the parentless, or those who are to be taught. Will the Lord have them in his holy care and keeping, and be gracious unto them, that on them may come the dew of heaven, and that they may blossom as in the garden of the Lord, and bring forth the fruit of righteousness.

We thank thee for the bounty of this day. We rejoice that the church has thus blossomed within as the world has blossomed without and filled all the fields with flowers. We thank thee for all the joy and hope and inspiration of this blessed morning.

And now we pray that thou wilt help us to strengthen one another's bonds by a holy sympathy and helpfulness. Help all that are young and are in our midst to grow up in manliness, in truth, in integrity, and in piety. Grant, we beseech of thee, that all the members of our households may dwell in the light of thy countenance. Even in sorrow let there be songs in the night for them. We pray that thou wilt establish thy covenant with every one of us, and do exceeding abundantly more for us than we ask or think, through Jesus Christ our Lord.

Accept our thanks for the mercy of the year.

We thank thee for the renewing tokens, month by month, of thy presence, of the vitality of the truth, and of the persuasions that are bringing men to a better life and restoring those that have wandered. And we pray that still, as the months go on, thy work in this congregation may continue, and abound, and bring forth more and more fruit to the glory of God.

We pray for thy blessing to rest, to-day, upon all thy churches in this city, and in the great city near us. We pray for all thy servants who minister in them, that they may be able to preach the Word with simplicity, with truth, and with power sent down from on high. We thank thee that differences are being laid aside, and that thy people work together better and more cordially than aforetime. We pray that divisions may be taken away, that walls of separation may be lowered, and that those things which tend toward inharmony may be abolished. May love everywhere prevail between thy people. May there be such sweet unity among them that men shall say, not, "How Christians hate one another!" but, "How they love one another!"

We pray that the power of truth may more and more ameliorate the condition of the people on this great continent. Raise up the weak, the ignorant and those that are trodden down as the mire in the street. We pray for all, everywhere, who are included under our government, that the light of civilization may come to them, if they be barbarous, and that they may be advanced in morality and knowledge wherever they may be. Rear up those who shall teach and those who shall preach the gospel, everywhere, that thy kingdom may come in all this great land.

Nor do we pray for ourselves alone: we pray for all the nations of the earth—especially for those that are more intimately connected with us on our great northern border, and those that are across the deep, from whom we sprang. O, God of nations, may we be knitted together more and more firmly for the cause of civilization, of Christian truth, and of universal elevation. We beseech of thee that thou wilt spread the light with growing clearness upon all the nations.

Lord, when shall the wolf go back to his den, and the lion cease to ravage? When shall the white banner of peace float over all the earth? How black and how red are now the flags of war! We pray that the tramp of the soldiers may cease, that the thunder of the cannon may be heard no more, that nations may no more learn war, that in knowledge there may be the destruction of superstition and despotism, that injustice may no longer excite men's passions, and that justice, and truth, and fidelity, and love may unite men, that the strength of the race may be expended not in going back to animalism, but in going forward and upward to morality and spirituality, until the prophecies shall be fulfilled and the earth shall see thy salvation.

Closing Prayer.

GIVE to us the light, unblemished, that shines from the heavenly sphere, our Father. Deliver us all from the temptations of mutual admirations, self-admirations, disguises, and self-deceit. Bring us, we beseech of thee, where thy servant of old was, who lived as seeing Him who is invisible. Give to our faith such a perpetual sense of the truth of the invisible that we may become evermore like Him. Bless those that are striving to-day, low down, and under all discouragements. Quicken their courage. Let them not fail. Give them, we beseech thee, by the Holy Ghost, power to overcome their quick and fiery adversaries, and to cast them down to the ground ; and make them feel that it is indeed heroic to slay Satan in every movement that he makes upon them. And may they work not discouraged, because of to-day, nor afraid of to-morrow. From day to day may they unweariedly take hold of the promise of God, and realize his presence, and behold the joy of purity in the immaculate Man ; and there may the vision abide, as a vision of angel faces, to comfort and cheer them in despondency, and to carry them on from height to height till their feet shall stand in Zion and before God.

Help the patient to be more patient. Help the struggling more perfectly to overcome, and to reap victory out of struggle. Help us all, Lord, for our days are few, and what we do we must do quickly. Help us by thine own immortal love. Set to us the example of what is heroic, that we may be followers of Christ indeed.

Invocation.

THOU high and holy One, thou who art lifted above all compare, though men are but as grasshoppers in thy sight, greatness with thee doth not lift thee above the poor and needy. Thou that dost deal mercifully with those who are of a humble and contrite spirit and of a broken heart, look down with infinite compassion upon us, who confess our sins and our unworthiness, and implore forgiveness in the name of our Lord Jesus Christ. Grant unto us the ministering power of thy Spirit, to-day. Let thy soul touch ours. Let thy life brood our drooping life, and bring forth out of our souls the bright resurrection morning in which all sweet thoughts and all heartfelt faith and love rise up to greet and to rejoice in thee. And may the services of the sanctuary, our meditation therein, the joy of home and the labors of love, this day, be sanctified and accepted by thee.

A Sabbath Day.

Sunday Morning, June 1, 1873.

WE thank thee, our Father, for this blessed day of rest. We pray that it may bring repose to all that are in trouble; to all that are sick; to all that are weary from watching hopelessly with the sick;

to all that are in great distress of mind; to all that are pestered; to all that are hindered. We pray that it may be a day of emancipation to all thy children who are held captive by ignoble care, or by any bondage or strife. Grant that this may be a day in which the heavens shall come down in brightness upon all the souls which thou hast made, as upon the outward world. May the truths of thy Word, the majesty of love in God, the power and redemption and sympathy in the heart of Christ, the enlightening and searching and reviving influence of the Holy Spirit, come to thy servants. May they not hold the truth in its letter, in its outwardness, and in the shackle of human thought and feeling and expression: may there be brought to them, by the Holy Ghost, to-day, revelations of the truth in its ineffable form; as it is outside of us; as it is in the sight of God.

Grant that we may behold the reality of time. May we behold its uses, and yet realize how little it avails as a rest or as a treasure. Grant that we may behold the glory of the invisible. May it be brought near—the incorruptible spirit; the unchangeable future; the great rejoicing-ground of the universe, whither, when men have blossomed, thou dost pluck them, and bear them up, and give them, where there is no winter, a place in which to grow again. Grant that we may all have a sense of the reality of God present with us to-day. May this be a Sunday full of God; and so, full of gladness, and hopefulness, and thanksgiving, and rejoicing one with another. We beseech of thee, to-day, that tears may cease, that cares may have their furrows smoothed out, and that every one may take his place as a child of God, and look up into the face of his Father, not to plead, but with smiles and humble boldness to demand that which love has agreed to give.

Wilt thou help every one, and make it easy for him to confess the wrong that is in him, and to loose the band that has hindered him and held him down, and rise with sweet approach to a consciousness and a realization of the love of God in Christ Jesus. Grant a knowledge of the infinite treasure that is in that love to every pilgrim soul upon earth. Thou art dealing with thy people. Thou art chastising many of them. Thou art calling them to walk in dark ways. Thou art putting the cup of bitterness to the lips of many. Thou art exercising them and training them for the better ground that is beyond. We pray that they may not be forsaken in the dark way. We pray that their night may not be starless. We pray that they may not cry out when they are drawing near to thee on the stormy sea as if they had seen a spirit: may they know in every deed that all their experiences are brought upon them by the hand of love; may they be strengthened to drink the cup; and, if it may not pass by them, may they have the angels of God ministering to them, and be led to lay all their cares and burdens of sorrow at the feet of the Saviour.

We pray for all those who know not what to do; for all those who desire to do their duty, but are perplexed by the opening of various ways. We beseech of thee that they may not lie supine, waiting for God to tell them. May they hear the voice of God demanding that they shall use their own reason to find out what their duty is; and then may they do the best they can and wait for that better light which shall come from following the light which they already have. And may those who are burdened and weighed down with care not be looking to see wherewithal they shall be relieved: may their cry still be for strength to bear their burdens and endure their cross. May those who are in the conflict of life not desire to retreat or to fall out by the way; but having done all, may they stand.

We ask that the Spirit of the mighty God may be in the hearts of his people, in their several relations to each other—in the household, in business, in the affairs of State, and in their connection with time and eternity. Grant that they may, every one, feel this morning the brooding influence of divine love in the certainty that all things shall work together for good to them that love God. May there be a childlike nature springing up in every heart, and reaching by thoughts and desires and hopes toward the spirit-land—toward the crown of immortal life.

We beseech of thee, O Lord our God, that thy Word to-day may fly speedily throughout this land. By thousands of preachers may the Word of God, and the love of Christ, and the hope of the world, be made known. May sluggish ears be aroused, and dead hearts revived, and multitudes brought out of darkness and into light. We pray for thy cause universal; for the diffusion of intelligence; for the emendation of law; for the establishment of righteous custom; for the spirit of integrity and purity, among this great people.

We pray for the nations that are enthralled. May their bonds be broken. May superstition be chased away by the knowledge of a better religion in Christ Jesus. May the weakness of men, which has made them the prey of the oppressor, disappear. May men be strengthened until oppression shall not be able to hold them down.

We pray for the fulfillment of those blessed predictions which promise the enlightenment of the whole world and the emancipation of the entire race. Even so, Lord Jesus, we wait upon thy word and upon thy promises. We are willing to wait, if need be, and to labor, sowing with tears, even, if by and by we may come to thee with our bosom filled with sheaves. And grant that we may come with abundant fruit as the result of faithful toil all our life long.

We pray that thou wilt bless those to-day that attempt to fulfill the duties which thou thyself didst fulfill upon earth, by going about doing good. May all who comfort the sorrowing be comforted themselves of God. May all that bear the torch of light be themselves enlightened. May all that lift up the lowly and encourage the despairing be themselves mightily blessed of God.

We leave ourselves in thy keeping. Do that with us which seems good to thee. Whether we live a longer or a shorter period, whether we are in one or another condition or place, grant that we may have evermore the presence of the Lord Jesus Christ, his grace, his love, his strength, his conscious sympathy, so that we shall be mighty to the pulling down of strongholds of sin. And at last bring us to that rest which remaineth for the people of God.

Closing Prayer.

THOU that givest the light, and quickenest all things by its stimulus, give the light and power of the Holy Ghost to the truth that has been uttered. May we bear it in thoughtful hearts, and with earnest purposes, into the fulfillment of daily life. Pardon all our sins. Save us from ourselves and from all other enemies. Deliver us in the hour of death, and bring us with a more glorious consummation into the eternity of blessedness in Thine upper kingdom, through riches of grace, in Christ Jesus.

Invocation.

LIFT upon us, our Father, the light of thy countenance. May that light come unobscured by winter, by storm or by trouble. Breathe forth upon us that peace of which thou art the Source and the sole Possessor. We are cast about upon these lower shores by every wind of care. Grant that we may know thy presence by its soothing influence, by the gentle incitement of our souls, by the warmth of love and by the holy thoughts inspired of thee. And may our services of instruction, of devotion, of fellowship and of rejoicing be acceptable in thy sight.

For Spiritual Discernment.

Sunday Morning, Dec. 16, 1877.

DELIVER us, our Father, from all those mists which do arise from the low places where we dwell, which rise up and hide the sun, and the stars even, and thee. Deliver us from the narrowness and the poverty of our conceptions. Deliver us from the despotism of our senses. And grant unto us, this morning, the effusion of thy Spirit, which shall bring us into the realm of spiritual things, so that we may, by the use of all that which is divine in us, rise into the sphere of thy thought, into the realm where thou dwellest, and whither have trooped from the ages the spirits of just men now made perfect. Grant, we pray thee, that we may not look with time-eyes upon eternal things, measuring and dwarfing with our imperfectness the fitness and beauty of things heavenly. So teach us to come into thy presence and to rise by sympathy into thy way of thinking and feeling, that so much as we can discern of the invisible may come to us aright. O deliver us, we beseech of thee, from those ways and estimates which grow out of life, from that importance which is transient, and from that carelessness of eternal things which we do so bear about with us, undervaluing the great over-realm, and being excessively addicted to that which is beneath our feet. We bend under heavy loads for the sake of gaining the things that are transient, thus periling the things which are eternal. We are earnest and laborious in our efforts to obtain the treasures of this world, while we are, perchance, indifferent to the eternal treasure.

O Lord, quicken us. May we lift our hands to our head for the crown that is ours. May our hand hold the scepter in which is all authority and power; and may we be able therewith to wave away or beat down the impertinences and falsenesses of this world. Remove all things that come

between us and the clear-seeing of the will of our
God, and of the estate of the ransomed, and the
royal company that are more ours since they went
from us than while they were with us. Then we
spoke to each other as through prison walls, en-
ccompassed in the flesh, bearing about a common
blindness and inaptness; but they have gone forth
to find themselves in the largeness of the spirit
world. With them, now, love flames as the sun of
the tropics; joy rolls in everlasting measures
with them; and they embrace with their souls the
whole wide world, and all that is in it. Their
thoughts follow Christ's, and they wing their way
every whither, and rejoice—especially with them
with whom they learned to weep, and with whom
they bore burdens.

O bring down the brooding heaven to us, if we
cannot rise into it, this day, that all those who seem
to themselves to have been losers may behold what
they have gained. None can lose except those
who are of the earth, earthy. Whatever we cast
downward is gone, and death owns it; but the
things which we cast upward, and for which men
mourn, we invest aright ; because death cannot
reach to take the things which we have committed
to thy trust.

We rejoice in that heaven where our little children are. We rejoice in that region where our much-stormed friends have gone. We rejoice in that land where the wicked cease from troubling and the weary are at rest. May we not have solicitude, may we not have solemnity, may we not have the fear and trembling of those that doubt; but O, this day, more than misers rejoice in counting their gold may we rejoice in counting the treasures that are laid up for us where moth and rust do not corrupt, and where thieves do not break through and steal. And whatever change and loss may betide our earthly possessions, may we walk in high and heavenly thought, not far from Him who redeemed us by his love, and through whom we have learned to magnify God.

Grant thy blessing to rest on all who are gathered together in thy presence this morning. May there seem to them to be a heavenly atmosphere in this place; and may they have freedom to open their hearts to the inshining of God's heart. As to-day nothing will grow under the sharp and biting influence of winter, but all things will open when the sun comes again from the south, with its warmth and blessed breath, so grant, we pray thee, that those hearts which have been congealed by care, by trouble, by fear, by the misconstruction of thy nature, of thy government and of thy purposes, may open their souls to the sweet influence of the mild and blessed love which streams from the face of joy. May they confess their sins to themselves, and to Him who alone loves enough to forgive; and grant that they may have rest in Christ to-day, not because they have done so much or meant so much, but because they find his mercies enwrapping them. May their strength and their gladness rest in what He is and not in what they are.

Grant, we pray thee, that all those who are in sorrow, all those who are bereaved, all those who are sick, all those who are in any trouble, and need comfort, may, to-day, have the consolation of the Comforter. We pray for those who are taxed beyond their strength and who long to lay down their burden. May they put on the whole armor of God, and having done all, may they be steadfast, and patiently endure unto the end.

May thy blessing rest upon the households of this congregation. Bless thy servants that are parents. Fill them with all Christ-likeness, and make their way before their children a perpetual gospel. May they learn of their children, and may their children learn of them. Bless the labor of thy servants who are at work in our schools and missions. Bless all the officers, all the teachers, and all that are taught. May thy servants not teach as if they felt that they were conferring a favor upon thee. The lowest place is too much honor for any one of us when we think who thou art, O Christ, in the glory of thy Father's kingdom. If we might but touch the hem of thy robes, and bear up thy train in the least, it would be an honor all too great. May there be an ever present humility among those who go forth to teach. May they deport themselves, not as though they were bestowing a benefaction upon inferiors. May a spirit of love and brotherhood go with them. And may they show such true manliness, such real magnanimity, such greatness of patience, such long-continued willingness to work unrequited, to be subordinate one to another, and to submit themselves to each other, that their scholars shall behold in them the meaning of that gospel which is of the heart, and not of the book.

Bless thou all who are present with us from abroad. Though they are strangers among strangers, may they yet find that they are in the household of faith, and at home. Grant that their prayers, commingling with ours, may go forth in answers to those that they have left behind. Preserve their families. Protect thy servants from evil in their wanderings, guard them, and in due time guide them again to their own.

Bless, we pray thee, this whole land, in all its interests. May a spirit of dispassionate wisdom in its rulers work truth and reason and success for the welfare of this great people. We pray for this nation, divided in many nationalities and conditions. Grant, we fervently beseech of thee, that we may cast away the distinctions that have tormented this country, and that we may believe that in Christ Jesus there is neither Jew nor Gentile, neither bond nor free, neither man nor woman, but that all are before thee alike. And in our hearts, in the greatness of our sympathy, and in the performance of all our duties, may we be able to rise to the spirit of Christ Jesus. We pray that thou wilt hasten the day when there shall be no ignorance, no domineering by the passions, no rude violence through selfishness, no craft nor deceit, no hatred. Grant that there may be union, not only external but internal, in this great nation, and that the memory of the past may be sanctified in the deeds of the future.

Yea, may all the nations of the earth rise in civilization, so that all oppressive governments, all corrupt practices, all superstitions, and everything that torments and vexes and destroys men, may be taken out of the way, and that those peoples that are yet in darkness may hear the trumpet call of God, and come trooping to his banner, and join the march of civilization and religion.

O Lord, we pray thee, hasten the consummation of thy purposes. Call forth from their hiding-places the children of the night. Bring to completion those counsels that have so long stood as prophecies. Make haste; for all the earth is waiting for thee, and generations sigh and yearn, and die without the sight. Come, thou Desire of nations, and make manifest in the fulfillment of thy promises the glory of God in the welfare of men.

Closing Prayer.

GOD grant that we may live in the faith of that which now we see not, in the hope of that which we desire. O Lord, help us to populate the future with all the glories of things longed for but not seen. Grant, we pray thee, to every one of us, in the instruction of the day, a wiser thought of our own way of life and our own way of duty. May we be helped, and taught how to help and not to hinder others. Purify this church. Make it strong in faith and wisdom and love. Purify all thy churches. Reveal thyself more and more to them. Teach them not to close their eyes when God is revealing the truth all the world around. May they rejoice, expecting evermore the second coming of Christ. Little by little rejoicing, may they live in the faith that He may yet possess the world.

Invocation.

DEAR Father, open our hearts that we may feel thy presence. We need no help to seek the light and warmth of the sun, so much more vital is the body than our soul; but thou Sun of righteousness, when thou comest we need thy help that we may know thee and feel thy power. Of all the gifts which thou hast for us none are like the gift of thine own self. And we pray, this morning, that we may know thy presence, not by any outward sign or symbol, but by the awaking in us of all that is affectionate and yearning of the higher and holier aspirations, that we may feel that leaning of soul which implies thee upon whom we may rest ourselves. And may all our service, to-day, begin and end in thee, that we may be surrounded by thee. Be thou all in all, and glorify thyself in the wonder of love, mercy, and gentleness in the midst of thy people.

Comfort in Prayer.

Sunday Morning, Jan. 20, 1878.

THOU, O God, hast exalted us so that no longer we walk with prone head among the animals that perish. Thou hast ordained us as thine own children, and hast planted within us that spiritual life which ever seeks, as the flame, to rise upward and mingle with thee. Every exaltation, every pure sentiment, all urgency of true affection, and all yearning after things higher and nobler, are testimonies of the divinity that is in us. These are the threads by which thou art drawing us away from sense, away from the earth, away from things coarse and unspiritual, and toward the ineffable. We rejoice that we have in us the witness of the Spirit, the indwelling of God. For, although we are temples defiled, though we are unworthy of such a Guest, and though we perpetually grieve thee, and drive thee from us, so that thou canst not do the mighty work that thou wouldst within us, yet we rejoice to believe that thou dost linger near us. Even upon the outside, thou standest knocking at the door until thy locks are wet with the night dews, and dost persuade us with the everlasting importunity of love, and draw us upward, whether with or without our own knowledge. Thou art evermore striving to imbue us with thyself, and to give us that divine nature which shall triumph over time and sense and matter; and we pray that we may have an enlightened understanding of this thy work in us and upon us, and work together with thee.

We thank thee for the glimpses that we have

had aforetime. We thank thee that there have been to us mountains of transfiguration. We thank thee that the heavens have opened to us, and that we have heard thy voice, that we have felt the descending Spirit, that it has rested upon us, and that the fire hath burned in our thought and in our soul. We thank thee, also, that thou hast given us the eye of the prophet, that the future is open, that we have pierced the darkness of the grave at times, that we have beheld the further shore across the Jordan, and that we have penetrated the realm beyond,—yea, and entered in, with blessed communion, to the rest which is found among the saints in glory. We thank thee that faith in us has prevision, and that we discern things which are to come, if not in their exact substance and figure, yet in such a way as brings comfort and refreshment to us while we are waiting; while we are pilgrims in the desert; while we are in tabernacles, and seek mansions and cities that are builded. We thank thee that we are cared for aforetime by thee, that thou dost succor and sustain us along the way.

And now we beseech of thee, O Lord, that the memory of the past may comfort us in all the future, when sorrows like swollen rivers, and like storms on the mountains, seem likely to sweep us away. May we remember the deliverances of old, and abide in faith. When the flame threatens to consume us, may we call to mind the times gone by when thou didst stand by us in the fire, and protect us. When the fear of death draws near, may we recollect thy words, that because thou hast overcome we shall overcome also. When it seems as though all our earthly hopes were blasted, may we acquit ourselves like men, and stand up in the midst ot trial and trouble, and bearing patiently the will of the Lord that is laid upon us, endure unto the end. For, what can happen amiss to those who are God's own children? What if the earth does melt beneath our feet! What if the comforts of outward life are taken from us! If thou art near us, and if the enduring riches that are forevermore at thy right hand are our inheritance, why should we be distressed and in pain? What if we seem solitary, deserted, abandoned! Is not ours the company of the general assembly and the church of the first-born; and can we be alone who are surrounded with clouds of witnesses, calling out to us in hope and in love?

Grant, we pray thee, that in the ministry of things spiritual and invisible we may find more than an equivalent for the trouble, the trial, of this visible world. It perishes, and the invisible endures forever. Here we groan, being burdened; but in the realm above sorrow and sighing shall flee away. There shall be no more tears there. The former things will have passed away. Since we are heritors of that blessed kingdom, walking crownless, and yet crowned the sons of God, and although we are obscure and unknown, grant that we may prove ourselves worthy of the high vocation with which we are called in Christ Jesus. O, thou that didst shed tears, thou that wert stained with blood, thou that wert crowned with thorns, thou of the pierced hand and side, interpret to us more perfectly the grandeur of that love which works within thy Father and our Father. May we understand the suffering God that for us bears care and burden and trouble. May we rejoice in the universality of thine overruling and succoring providence, and of the gospel that works within it. And so we pray that we may be stable unto the very end.

Bless, we pray thee, all that are in thy presence, and each as he needs, with patience, with strength, with humility, with gentleness, with generosity, and with disinterested love and service. Minister to those who are in the twilight. Bring the day-star to watchers in the night. May those who are in anguish, and whose hearts quiver, feel thy heart, and take medicine from it. Do to every one such things as shall enable him every day, with the enthusiasm of love, to say, Our Father. And may thy name be as a talisman, and guard us and guide us and bless us.

And we pray not only for ourselves, but for all—for those that are not permitted to be with us to-day; for those that are sick at home; for those that are upon the sea; for those that are in foreign lands; for those that are in the wilderness in our own land; for those who are in our army and navy; for those who are laboring for the amelioration of the condition of the people; for ministers of the gospel; for those who conduct institutions of learning; and for editors that diffuse light and knowledge throughout the nations.

We pray that thou wilt bless the President of these United States and those that are joined with him in authority. Bless the Congress assembled, all legislatures, all courts, all judges, magistrates of every name, and the whole citizenship of this broad land. Breathe thou a spirit of wisdom and unity and integrity upon our great people, and lead them forth aright.

And we pray that thou wilt grant, not to ourselves alone, but to all the nations of the earth, peace and prosperity. Open the future; bring in the promised joy; cut short the lingering and hesitating steps; and advance with strength those that bring salvation. How beautiful upon the mountains are the feet of those that bring good tidings of peace to the world! And what world ever needed such tidings as this one, which yet groans and travails in pain!

Now, Lord, we commend ourselves again to thy care, asking thy blessing, thy spiritual guidance, through all the scenes of this life, and through the last, death, and into the eternal home; and there we will give the praise of our salvation to the Father, the Son, and the Spirit, evermore.

Closing Prayer.

GRANT unto us, we pray thee, the spirit of thy word. It is filled with sweet fruit, and sweet perfume. We thank thee, O God, that thy book is full of life, and that the notes of sadness in it are but distant echoes; whereas the joy overflows, chorally and continuously. So make us rejoice in the Lord, that, by trust, by hope, by love, we may come into that atmosphere from which winter is expelled, and in which summer dwells forevermore.

Invocation.

THOU divine Spirit, look forth unto our humble estate; and as thou wert not ashamed, once, to descend and to be born of a woman, and to make thyself altogether acquainted with human grief, so vouchsafe from thy great glory to descend again and again, to be incarnated in us, to dwell in us, and to give us thy life and thy love. And may we feel within us, to-day, that inspiration which shall be the token and evidence of thy presence. May our service be acceptable, though it be poor, as the best that we know how to bring; and may we, this day, from thy Word, gain new light, new motive, and new impulse, so that the service shall not be unprofitable to us and shall be grateful to thee.

The Wonders of Grace.

ACCEPT our songs of thanksgiving and of praise, O thou Most High. Unworthy of thee they are; and yet, how shall we, at this distance, being so imperfect, and beholding through clouds and darkness, celebrate the full glory of thy heavenly estate? What can we do but that which is done in weakness and imperfection? Yet it is not that which we utter, but that which through Jesus Christ is brought unto thee, that thou dost hear. Thou dost interpret our broken language. Thou dost give significance to that which we say, and make it that which we would utter, and not that which we do.

We rejoice that we have thus in the heavenly sphere One who stands for us—a Forerunner, a Mediator, a Saviour, a beloved Friend, who has been joined to us, who knows our every infirmity; who is united to thee, who is familiar with every perfection; who brings us into relation with thee, and who gives us possession of our own selves in our nature, in our destiny, in our true and divine element.

And so, though we praise thee with insignificant word, and incompetent thought, and inadequate conception, thou art pleased to receive us and ours, and dost rejoice in us and over us. This is the marvel of grace: how out of thy greatness thou canst take pleasure in littleness; how out of thy great purity thou canst look with compassion upon the impure; how out of thine ineffable perfection thou canst have sympathy with the imperfect—yea, dost love them; for it is thou that didst set the root agrowing, and it is thou that didst give to the sprouting seed its rudest form as well as its final blossom.

All through thou art pleased with the growths and disclosures of things; under thy care the earth is evermore working upward; in each generation thou dost move things back to the beginnings; and thou dost call forth the soul on its march from imperfection toward perfection. Thou hast some design in thine own mind, although we cannot pierce to understand it. Though we do not know what are its relationships, though we are ignorant of what are the plans and purposes of our God, we are glad to believe that thou art such an One as can take compassion upon our infirmities; that thou dost pity us because thou knowest our frame, and dost remember that we are dust, so that our very want and our very weakness bring us near to thee, to thine illumination, and to thy healing power. So thou art revealing to all thy creatures, above and below, that thy nature is to heal, and to strengthen, and to build up; that it is thy nature to be patient and long-suffering; that it is thy nature, with firm and steady pressure, with skill and with fidelity, to develop us until we are perfected and made ready for the sphere above.

In the faith of this we desire, O Lord our God, to rejoice, and to walk day by day, not dependent upon our own condition, but dependent upon our God, and made strong in the hope of his salvation.

Grant thy blessing to abide with all the households in this church; and may every family be itself a church. May there be a church in each house. We pray for the ministration of the Spirit upon the parents, and upon the children and the little ones. May the young grow up in purity, in honor, in truth, in perfect manhood in Christ Jesus. Bless thy servants in their relations to the outward world; in their duties; in their various intercourse with men; in their ambitions and hopes of worldly good; in their joys and sorrows; in their defeats and victories. Will the Lord make them to be Christian men in disposition and in conduct.

To such as are in trouble give release, or give them support. Take away their hindrance, or bear them up under it by thy strength. Bless, we beseech of thee, any that are sick. Comfort them, restore them, or bring them through, with final victory, to the home of the Lord Jesus Christ. If any sit in darkness, and mourn through bereavements, wilt thou come unto them, though thou hast delayed thy coming, and cheer and comfort them, as thou didst the sisters of old.

May thy blessing rest upon those present who are strangers in a strange land or in a strange place. May they find here a home of the soul;

and in communion with God and his people may they find rest from care and anxiety, and refreshment as of food in thy holy Word; may this place and this sanctuary be greatly blessed to their souls.

We pray that thou wilt follow our thoughts of yearning love to all, everywhere, who are dear to us, in our own or in other lands, upon the sea or upon the soil. Wherever they may be, we commend them to thy fatherly care and protection. Shower upon them abundant blessings, we pray thee; and may the memories of this place which shall arise in a thousand hearts to-day be sanctified, so that this day shall be to all that are scattered abroad who belong to us a day of rest and rejoicing.

Bless, we pray thee, the city in which we dwell. Establish thou righteousness in it. Cleanse it, purify it, and make it strong in the things that make for peace and justice and truth. Bless our whole land. We thank thee that the troubles which threatened great mischief and disaster are passing away; we thank thee that there was so little harm where there was fear of so much; and we pray that thou wilt give to us more and more assured laws, wise administration, and perfect obedience. Deliver us from the passions of evil men, from rancor, from envy, from hatred, from envenomed contentions; and may this great people dwell together in peace.

Closing Prayer.

OUR Father, wilt thou bless thy truth as unfolded. May it do good. Wilt thou give help to those who need help ; a clearer light to those who are in darkness and doubt ; a fountain of life to those who are in the valley and shadow of death. We pray that thou wilt help men to break away from their evil habits, and to enter upon a nobler life and character. Wilt thou glorify thyself in that which thy people bring forth. May men go from grace to grace and from virtue to virtue until they become men in Jesus Christ. And may they live so that men around about them shall behold their light, their strength, their gladness and beauty, and shall glorify their Father which is in heaven.

Invocation.

BECAUSE thou art good, and because thou hast called unto our souls, we have come to appear in Zion and before God. Now, what wait we for? Open thine arms for us. Give forth from thine heart that inspiration which shall make everything in us rise up and recognize our filial relation. With all our hearts and souls, may we be able to call thee our Father, and, this day, to rejoice somewhat in the contemplation of that realm of righteousness and wealth of joy which thou hast for thine own self and for all that are heirs through Jesus Christ of thy great salvation. Help us in every service. Make us, to-day, as joyful as thou wouldst have us to be.

The Sympathy of God.

WE thank thee, our Father, that it is permitted us, not only to think of thee, to be conscious of thy footsteps near us, to feel the touch of thy creating nature, everywhere, but to speak of thee, to commune with thee; and though we do not discern thy face, though we do not feel the pressure of thy hand, and though thou canst not be a Father to us in the flesh as our fathers were, yet we rejoice that inwardly we may know thy presence, that we may feel the power of thy Spirit working upon our spirits, and that we may have that feeling of exaltation, that sensibility to things invisible, that love of things noble and right, which shows us to have gone out from under the dominion of outward elements, and to have come into the presence of the All-loving, of the All-powerful, of the All-knowing.

We rejoice that in all time men have found a refuge in thee, and that prayer is the voice of love, the voice of fear, the voice of pleading, and the voice of thanksgiving. Our souls overflow toward thee like a cup when full; nor can we forbear; nor shall we search to see if our prayers have been registered, or whether of the things asked we have received much, or more, or anything. That we have had permission to feel in thy presence, to take upon ourselves something of the light of thy countenance, to have a consciousness that thy thoughts are upon us, to experience the inspiration of the Holy Ghost in any measure —this is an answer to prayer transcending all things that we can think of; for what are all things in time but gifts of the Holy Ghost for the exaltation of our whole nature for eternity? We thank thee that we have thus more than an answer to our prayers, and that thou dost exceeding abundantly more than we can ask or think. Thou art acting in larger spheres than our desires ever compass. Thou art working out in us ends about which we do not ourselves know. It doth not yet appear to us what we shall be; but thou dost discern clearly that which we see in a glass, darkly. The veil has not fallen, and will not fall until death shall take it down.

We rejoice to believe that in the great sphere of thy beneficence thou art multiplying answers to our petitions; yea, and art sending to us flocks, as it were, of message-birds, bringing both song and food for the famished. Thou art rejoiced to do for us even unrecognized things innumerable.

And now we take hold upon thee, this morning, by hands of faith. O Lord, we stretch up to thee our feeble affection, knowing that it is pleasant to thee, and that anything which we can do in the spirit of love pleases thee. Unrich, we give to thee all that we have, knowing that anything which we can give shall be as riches to thee. And we have learned the secret of thy feelings, though we cannot understand it or take in its scope. Are not our little children a joy and a blessing to us, though we are above them in strength and in knowledge? And so we are glad to think that in the mystery of love thou canst take from us what we have to offer, though we are so poor, so distant from thee, and so infinitely beneath thee in every attribute and power of life. We are glad that we can enrich thee, that we can glorify thee, that we can rejoice thee, that it does make a difference to thee what we do, and that thou dost enfold us in a consciousness of thy sympathy with us, of how much thou art to us, and of what we are to thee.

Thou that hast loved and hast expressed thy love by giving to the uttermost whatsoever thou hadst,—thy throne, thine estate of glory and thine earthly life,—O grant that we may not doubt, that at least we may reach up so far as not to doubt, that He who hath given all things for our sake will freely give us whatever is needed for the warfare of life, for the victory of death, and for our translation to the heavenly kingdom!

Grant, we pray thee, to thy servants who are in thy presence this morning, a blessing according as they severally need, at home, in their business, in their triumphs, in their difficulties, in their burdens, in their experiences of anguish and settled sorrow, and gloom, and despondency, or in their new-blown joys, in their hopes, in their anticipations, in all the wide reach of their various soul experience. O Thou that dost refresh the weary, and renew their strength as the eagle's, grant unto every one in thy presence the morning's blessing and the day's bounty ; and may this day be one of the days of the Son of man to every one of us.

Grant thy blessing to rest upon all that labor in word and doctrine among us. May their lives be more and more sanctified. May their courage be increased continually. May they grow not alone in outward attainments, but in the spirit of Christ, and show forth that Spirit wherever they go. Bless our schools and missions. Remember their officers, their teachers, and all the pupils that are gathered unto them. Will the Lord have them in his holy care and keeping, by day and by night, by week-day and by Sabbath. May thy blessing rest upon all those who are seeking to understand the scope of charity, and are endeavoring to supply the wants of the poor and needy. Wilt thou bless those that visit jails and hospitals, and those that go forth into the highways and byways, to make known the unsearchable riches of Christ Jesus.

We pray that thou wilt bless all our magistrates, all our judges, all that bear authority, and all that perform for the community the necessary functions of government. Bless the whole body of citizens. May knowledge prevail everywhere.

May all that is base be more and more thoroughly trodden under foot. May that which is divine in humanity mingle in the government and council of our nation. May this great people, that in outward prosperity is set above all others, stand also clothed in equity and humanity, as well as liberty; may it be a bright example to the struggling nations of the earth; and may they, following this example as set by our fathers, become commonwealths founded upon the fear of the Lord, and upon his testimonies.

Closing Prayer.

OUR heavenly Father, we pray for those who are imperilled by temptation. We pray for those whose feet are sliding in a slippery way. We pray for those who are beginning to be discouraged in their efforts to reform. O God, forget not the downfalling! We pray for the outcasts whom all men have forgotten. We pray for the elevation of those whom all society hates. We pray that men may be taken out from under the hoof and put upon their feet again. Grant that more and more the spirit of love may rule in us and regulate our outward life. Purify our households, working out in us towards others that divine sympathy which thou hast towards us. Let thy kingdom come and thy will be done, on earth as it is in heaven.

Invocation.

POUR forth thine own self, thou eternal Creator, God and Father; for thou art infinite. There is no measuring the bounds of thy being. Thy breath is the life of the universe. Looking upon us, thou canst bless us with a spiritual help, with the atmosphere of heaven, without diminishing that which is for all thine host throughout thine infinite realm. Enough and to spare is there in our Father's house; and why should we go hungry and thirsty and faint, whose Lord is the God Jehovah! Vouchsafe to us, then, some token of the sweetness of thy power and of the greatness of thy love, transforming in us thy thought upon ours. May our hearts feel the waves that beat in from thy heart upon the shores of time. And in thy house, where thou hast wrought for many years great mercies upon our souls, again, this day, O thou loving and all-sufficient Saviour, pour forth the fruit of thy grace, that we may abound therein, and be rich in the everlasting life, through Jesus Christ, our Lord.

At the Close of a Year.

WE rejoice, our Father, that thou hast taught us that there remaineth a rest for the people of God; that this life is not all of our experience; that beyond the bounds of time swells the infinite, the eternal life. Thou art gathering there multitudes which no man can number. From every age thou hast garnered there; the spirits of the just made perfect dwell with thee, and thitherward set the streams of time. For us there is this hope and this joyful anticipation. We rejoice that the burdens which we bear, and the sorrows, the troubles, and the vexations of life which we experience day by day, are things to be forgotten; that they are but the dust of the way. Though at the time they fill the soul, and absorb the thought, yet we rejoice that they are trifles, and are not worthy to be mentioned in comparison with the exceeding and eternal weight of glory which is reserved for those who love and fear thee. And we beseech of thee that we may be able to live this life in the body with a constant faith of the great life of the spirit; that we may never be discouraged nor beaten down; that we may know that we are the King's sons. Though exiled, and in disguise, and in poverty, and even cast into shame, may we remember our birthright, the treasure that awaits us, the crown, the throne, the scepter, the glory of immortal and perpetual youth, where thou art. When the former things shall have passed away, when sorrow and dying shall

AT THE CLOSE OF A YEAR.

have fled, when thou shalt have wiped the tear from every eye, and when thou dost comfort us even as a father comforteth his child, then, in that blessed land where thou dwellest, what will be the memory of the troubles which we have had upon earth!

Grant that now we may be made brave by the anticipation of these things through faith. May we carry our trouble, our load, whatever it may be, patiently, strengthened by thee, and rejoicing in thee. May we seek every day more and more thy favor. May our life be hid in thine. May our purposes be, not those which roll along the dusty road of time, but those which take hold on immortality and glory.

As the years go by, and as the signs and tokens of departure come to us, may we be more earnest for the things that do not perish, and less and less held by the things that do. Help us in all things to be steadfast, immovable, always abounding in the work of the Lord. Though others reel to and fro, may we stand in thy strength. Though others are confused and perplexed, may we abide in peace beneath the shadow of thy wings. Though others are bereaved and in great sorrows, may we hear thee saying to us, No affliction is for the present joyous but grievous, yet afterward it shall work the peaceable fruit of righteousness unto them that are exercised thereby.

Grant unto us, in these declining hours of the year, such suitable meditations as shall make us better fitted for the year that is advancing to us. May we seek more earnestly the things that are high, and worthy of us, and less and less the things that perish in the using. And may thy word give us instruction. May it be the man of our counsel and our guide. We pray that its wisdom and experience may become our wisdom and experience, and that in it we may abide as in a fortress.

Grant, O Lord, thy blessing upon all those whose pilgrimage is beginning, who are essaying their first steps in the higher life. Deliver them from every enemy that threatens them from without; from the enemies that are within their own hearts; from the evils by which they are surrounded; from specious reasonings of every kind; from deceitful temptations; from all guile that would spoil their simplicity. Deliver them from everything that tends to destroy the nobility of Christian manhood. May they prove all things, and hold fast the things that are good, living better than we have lived before them, with more aspiration and with more attainments.

May thy blessing rest upon the year that is past.

Grant that the seed which has been sown by thy servants in this church may not perish. Though the winter storms beat upon it may it come forth in the spring and bear fruit a hundredfold. We pray that the fruits which have been gathered may be but first-fruits; and may we see from month to month throughout the coming year the blessing of the Lord resting upon the labors of days gone by.

Wilt thou bless all those who are teachers; all those who are ministers of mercy and consolation to the afflicted; all those everywhere who are building up waste places. Revive thy work in thy churches. Grant, we pray thee, that with the expiring year faults may expire, on the right hand and on the left; and in the coming year may there be a new record of righteousness. More and more may the power of God be manifest in the affairs of men. May thy kingdom come, and may thy will be done, upon earth as it is done in heaven. We ask it in the name of Jesus, our master, to whom, with the Father and the Spirit, shall be everlasting praises. *Amen.*

Closing Prayer.

OUR Father, wilt thou teach us to gain wisdom by looking at the past. And grant that we may be enabled, in looking forward, to see the thing that is best. We pray that we may not be vain-glorious. May we not be man-worshipers. May we see thee above human things and national affairs. May we behold thee leading on this nation by the feet and hands of all its children on every side. May we rejoice at the multiplicity of national influences which are at work among us. O may we not forget the wisdom of our fathers. And since by it thou hast chiefly founded our institutions, we pray that we may not change it for any influences which shall tend to weakness, and luxury, and effeminacy, and monarchy. We pray more and more for this great people that they may be built up in self-respect, in purity, in intelligence, in self-government, in love of the common weal, and in willingness to sacrifice themselves for the public good.

And now we pray that thou wilt bless us when we sing again to thy praise. Then may we go home to rejoice in all the goodness of God to us in the past. And at last bring us to our Father's house on high, where we will praise thee forever and forever.

Invocation.

ALREADY thou hast blessed us with the rising light both of the sun without and of the sun within, our Father, as in this place, made dear by a thousand memories, thou art come again to grant to us a sense of thy presence, the joy of thy salvation, that peace which betokens thy presence, and thine overshadowing, in which is all power. Help us to tread under foot trouble and trial; and this day may we stand as the King's sons, crowned with joy. May the services of the sanctuary please thee. May we be in sweet fellowship with each other. Let all bitterness and darkness be taken away. As the children of light and of joy may we come forth into liberty this day.

God's Presence.

O LORD, our God, we draw near to thee this evening not as beggars to the princely house where they have received doles in days gone by. Thou knowest what we have need of, before we ask of thee, better than we do. Thou only knowest what is best, thou Heart of hearts. Thine hand is large and liberal. Thy thoughts are more generous than our desires could make them. Thou art before us evermore; and we walk in thy footsteps. We come to thee that we may feel our souls warmed by the sympathy of thy heart; that we may be able to say, Our Father; that heaven may seem to us our home; that we may not be strangers far away evermore, but children, crying, Abba,—Father.

So grant to us, this evening, access through thy Spirit in us and upon us. Thou canst inspire us, if thou wilt, to do the things that are highest. We need thy help—light for blind eyes and hearing for deaf ears.

Grant unto us, we beseech of thee, something of thyself to-night, that we may realize the worshiping privileges which we have, the hopes which spring from thy word, and the confidence which comes from thy promises. May we, this evening, feel that we have come home to God, to the Saviour of the soul, to the light and inspiration of the spirit; and may it be good for us to dwell together for the hour in this holy place. How sacred thou hast made it! How much of our life has been woven here! How much of all that which gives us strength in health or sickness have we derived from this fountain into which angels help us to descend at the stirring of the waters! We thank thee for the past. We humbly trust thee for the future. We rejoice in thee evermore. We desire that our lives may seem to us not in ourselves but in thee; and that we may live by faith in Him who loved us, and gave himself for us.

Father, we are to-night in special need of thee. Vouchsafe to us, we pray thee, thy presence. If any faint, and their courage fail, may they remember that God fainteth not. May they behold the earth, the heaven, all creation, as their guardian. May they not trust themselves and those around about them. Grant that the sense of thy presence may bring peace and rest to us this evening. If there be those that are mourning over evils that cannot be repaired, if there be those that look upon their own lives deeply stained with sin, if there be those who see that their dispositions are wrenched asunder, and controlled, O thou that dost bring health to sickness, and strength to weakness, and hope to despair, appear to them. Bless those who are in prison. Make thy power manifest among thy people, to forgive sins not only, but to heal. May there be some sent away to-night with the blessing, Peace; thy faith hath made thee whole. May there be some that shall learn to trust Him who is the Author of their faith, and the Finisher thereof, who lives to love, and who loves to heal, and to make pure and perfect those that cast themselves upon him. May there be some souls that to-night shall give their hearts to the Lord Jesus Christ. We pray that thou wouldst bring in, from time to time, those that hunger and thirst after righteousness. May the royal bread and water of life be abundantly supplied to them. Bring them, we pray thee, to that bread and to that water which forever shall satisfy their hunger and quench their thirst.

We thank thee for so many as have been brought to thee here, and are now witnesses of thy sustaining grace in heavenly places through Christ Jesus. Lord, multiply the number of those who shall fill the places of those who are gone. As one and another wait for the summons, impatient to go and be with Christ, which is better than life, grant that there may be others brought forward to fill their places.

May this church be a fountain of consolation. Multiply its influences for good. Revive thy work in our midst; may we see men flocking to the throne of grace; and may we build for thine own honor and glory, that the power of the gospel may not seem misspent, and vain, but stronger than ever, and more fruitful.

Closing Prayer.

GRANT thy blessing, our Father, to rest upon the word spoken; and may it be a word to every one of us—a seed planted; and may the harvest, near and far, be abundant.

Invocation.

GIVE to us, our Father, that illumination by which we shall rise from the flesh and from things visible and material, to the realm of thought and feeling—even into the great invisible world around about us, where thou art, where spirits dwell, and to which we hasten. Grant, this morning, that we may have communion by the soul with thee. Cleanse and give sight to our darkened eyes, and life to our dullness; and grant that in all services of the sanctuary we may have the joy that comes from the blessing of thy love. Grant that in the reading of thy Word, and in listening to it, in meditation, in the fellowship of song and in the communion of prayer, we may be divinely led and blessed, through Jesus Christ our Lord.

The Greater Life.

WE do not humble ourselves before thee, our Father. We are sorry for our sins, but we are made lower than thou art, and we are not sorry for our inferiority. That we do not love thee to the measure of our capacity is our grief. That our purposes are so easily overwhelmed is our sorrow. That we are so open to incitements that move our lower life, and so dull to those that come upon the soul in the greatness of its strength, is our grief and sorrow day by day. Yet we contest, we fight, and we believe that in the end we shall be conquerors and more than conquerors through Him that loved us. We go on every day with our conflict, still praying, and yet believing that finally we shall overcome and sit down in thy kingdom.

We desire to bear this thought of sanctity in our affairs. We desire to feel that things which are the least, which are the most remote from observation, and which have no value in the eyes of this world, are part and parcel of that great movement by which we are ascending from the lower to the higher spheres, from the life of the body to the life of the spirit, and to the worship of God. While we rejoice to pluck the flowers that thou hast caused to grow plentifully along the way of our feet, while we are grateful for the fruit that hangs down for our need, yet, O Lord our God, we desire to feel that this is not our home; that the world is not our abiding-place; that we are strangers and pilgrims in this sphere; that we are hastening through it; and that our real home is with God, and with the heavenly host. May we not count ourselves unworthy of this greater life. Though we be in poverty here, though we be in degradation or disesteem, though we be neglected or in contempt, we desire to forget never that we are sons of God. In the midst of suffering and trial and conflict, and all the things that men call disasters, we still desire to walk worthy of our vocation. Be pleased to give us this inward strength. Gird us every day for the conflict of life. Give us patience every day. Give us faith and insight every day. Every day give us courage and hope, and some song of rejoicing. Though our feet be in fetters, though the prison be closed around about us, and the guards be set over us, may we sing songs in the night, and find an angel of deliverance.

We pray that our whole life, though it must be a life of conflict, may be a life of ascending, so that by and by, in years to come, we may stand on heights of experience, looking forth as from the land of Beulah, and discerning the sacred city. Though we cannot with our ears hear the songs of the redeemed, yet in our hearts we discern them— we know their welcoming call.

Grant, we pray thee, that we may live as seeing Him who is invisible, the Prince of Love, the Glory and Joy of Heaven, the soul's Liberator, our Redeemer and Leader.

All the world is nothing without thee. Thou art all in all. May we discern thee, and with growing apprehension, as the days move on, until thy will is accomplished, and we know that we have fulfilled the purposes of our God upon earth. Then, quicker than birds rise in autumn and fly to everlasting summer, may we lift ourselves up, and fly away, and be at rest, and join the great congregation, the multitude of the redeemed in the heavenly city, where there shall be no more sickness, no more sorrow, no more sin, and where God shall lovingly embrace each one, even as the mother embraces the child that is grieved, and wipe the tears from every eye.

Closing Prayer.

OUR Father, forgive our feebleness and our cowardice, forgive us that we should be so soon drawn aside from the great things of thy kingdom to the interests of our minor lives. Give us that exaltation of spirit which shall abide. Give us such hearts that we can rejoice in suffering, yea, and make up that which is lacking in Christ, in our own bodies. We pray that thou wilt look upon the strifes of men. At least wilt thou interpret the meanings of them to thy people. Look upon those that in weakness and want are struggling, they know not how nor by what ways, to reach where the air is pure, and where manhood can live. Be on the side of the poor. Be on the side of the wronged and the outraged. Smite the tyrant, and destroy tyranny. Bring in the shining light of knowledge and intelligence. O God, be thou the God of the people; and let all the earth praise thee.

Invocation.

ALMIGHTY GOD, thou hast met us in this place full often; and here, in contemplation, or in sacred song, or in the knowledge of thy truth, thou hast revealed thyself to us—to us personally, in our wants, in our necessities, in our aspirations, and in our desires, adapting thyself to our need. We come again, since we are always necessitous, and are invoked of thee to come in every time of need, but to give thanks; to rejoice in thy praise; to feel the reality of thine existence; to take hold of something higher than things seen, and refresh ourselves with the communion of those who are gone before. Grant that everything which shall hinder this rising of the soul above its circumstances in the body may be taken away. May all that carry trouble take hope. Rise thou, as the sun out of the sea to the weary mariner, in the clear heaven, and shine abroad, Sun of righteousness, with glory and healing in thy beams.

God's Fatherliness.

Sunday Morning, March 9, 1879.

UP through the multitude of thy mercies we raise our thoughts, O Lord our Father. By that which we have learned of love and care from our earthly parents we conceive something of thy goodness; but what man hath lived that was not filled with imperfection ! What is there upon the earth of parentage so disinterested and so full of power, of goodness, of understanding, and of all beauty and excellence as to be fit to represent thee and the grandeur of thine infinite nature ! But when thou hast taught us that thou art a Father, we bring to the conception of thy nature all that which we have learned in the household of love and fidelity; and we hear thee saying, " If ye, being evil, know how to give good gifts to your children, how much more shall your Father which is in heaven know how to give good things to them that ask him !" All the amplitude of that grand estate which is vouchsafed to man is thine. All the seasons roll forevermore in thee. All the outstretch of knowledge and wisdom and goodness, all of tenderness and beauty, are wrapped up in thee. Thou art the cause of everything that men admire, and love, and desire, and hope for. In thee is the kingdom of heaven. Thou art filled with all the treasures of goodness. Thou art to us a Father. Thou hast called us not sons only, but heirs. We inherit. We are going toward the eternal, the treasure-house of eternity. We are advancing from poverty to riches, from weakness to strength, from being unknown to knowledge and to glory. We are now struggling, that are to be victorious. We are now veiled, that are to shine with open face in the full luster of the glory of God. We are often cast down, that never again shall know weakness. We are making battle that we may have the everlasting victory. Through tears, through darkness, through sorrows, through all manner of self-reproach, we are lifting up the eye of faith toward that future when we shall know ourselves as we are known, and be as the angels of God. Blessed be thy name, that we may look up through all the distemperatures of life! As the end and aim of our very being may we live toward glory and honor and immortality. May it be ours to aspire to be in intimate communion with thee, that we may never be separated from thee.

Having loved thine own, thou lovest them unto the end; where thou art there they shall be; and we comfort ourselves in this knowledge. Not that we are wise, but that thou art wise. Not that we are strong, but that thou art almighty. Not that we are good, but that thy grace is more than sufficient for whatever is evil in us. We live in thy lenity and forgiveness; in thy mercy, which is *tender* mercy; in thy kindness, which is *loving* kindness.

And now, accept our thanks for all these hopes. May they breed·in us more and more cheerfulness and patience. More and more may we lift up to thee thankful and worshipful hearts. Give us, this morning, the spirit of devotion. May we join in the songs of those that forever rejoice in thee. May we cast out that sorrow and that grief which are treason to hope, that we may this morning soar upward higher than birds that sing in the air. May we as out of the branches of the tree of life sing to-day with joy in our hearts. We pray that thou wilt grant to us the faith of sons; and may we from this time forth renew our strength, and walk in all the way of the Lord blameless.

Bless, we pray thee, all who are in thy presence, according to their circumstances and conditions. Bless the aged. Bless those that are in the midst of the battle of life. Bless the young. Bless the little children. Will the Lord be gracious to them all. We pray that thou wilt day by day meet the exigencies of life by thy providence; and when all outward help seems to fail, and trouble surrounds us like night, grant that then we may be strong in the Lord, when we are not able to be strong in ourselves; and may we hope in the Lord, and rejoice in the Lord.

Bless, we pray thee, all the schools that are connected with this church, all its missions and all its labors. We pray that thou wilt sanctify all the officers of our schools and missions, the teachers, and all that go out to make known the gospel of Jesus Christ. We pray that thou wilt take away from this people vanity, and pride, and self-seeking, and vain-glory. May they be humble and gentle. May they put on the Lord Jesus Christ. May they not envy one another, nor any others. And we pray that by their holy lives, by the sweetness of their disposition, and by their Christ-likeness everywhere, they may gain final victory.

Closing Prayer.

WE beseech of thee, O God, that thou wilt look forth from out of thine eternity of light ; for there love dwelleth, and giveth light and joy. Bless us in our despoiled condition, helpless, captive, yet praying, and reaching up our hands for deliverance. Have compassion upon us, this morning, not according to our deserving, but according to the abundant riches of thy goodness. Vouchsafe to us that inspiration which shall enable us to receive the light of truth from out thy Word. Thou that didst, upon the day which this day celebrates, come forth thyself from sleep and the grave, to give light and life to the world, bring thou the spirit of truth forth from the death of the letter to us, with a joyful resurrection of life for the soul.

Invocation.

VOUCHSAFE, not from afar off, but near unto us, O Lord our God, thy blessing, which comes from thine inshining. We are not to cry to thee as if thou wert at a distance. Heaven is not a long way from us. Thy thoughts run very swiftly. Or, if we know our own thought or our own feeling, behold thou art close at hand. We draw toward thee, this morning, asking that we may feel thy nearness, and that by the power of the Holy Ghost we may be lifted above the conceptions of our bodies, and into that realm of the soul with which thou dost hold communion, and that we may be there as dear children, and thou as the beloved Head and Father. So, God, may thy grace be unto us, and the service of the day be blessed and memorable, to thine honor and glory.

The Dullness of Earthly Vision.

O LORD our God, in the midst of praise and gladness thou art not forgetful of those that dwell in weakness and in the shadow of life. We are beginners—babes; but thy heart is as a mother's, and, whatever else in the household may be forgotten, never the child! Whatever angels may be about thee, whatever royal decrees may go forth in majesty to their execution, and whatever may be the pomp, the triumph and the rejoicing around about the heavenly sphere, the earth is not forgotten. Its sorrows, its various trials, are all before thee. Thou dost bear us in perpetual remembrance. And we rejoice in this sovereignty of love, in this sympathy of love, in this ever-presence and omniscience of love. It is our hope, as it is our life.

But we are glad that all is not as we see it. We are glad that around about us and near to us there go forth incessantly so many joys and so many songs of triumph. We rejoice that there are such victories that shall know no more overthrow. We rejoice that there is a rest undisturbed by sin or by want, near to us, just above us. Were we not encased in the flesh we should hear the holy conversation of the upper realm. Were not these eyes of the body too much dulled, we should behold the endless throngs that surround us—the assembly of the just, the angels ministrant, the church triumphant. With all our hearts we should enter into the communion of the saints. While yet upon the earth we should speak to those that are in the heavenly sphere. But though these opaque bodies let nothing shine through them, we rejoice in the preciousness of the thought of what is beyond. And we beseech of thee, O Lord our God, that thou wouldst grant unto us more and more of that faith which overcomes the world and sin. Grant unto us that holy hope which shall cheer us in the midst of despondencies and troubles.

May thy blessing, this morning, rest upon thy servants who are gathered together here. Who shall read the open book of life? Not they that bear joy know what that joy means. Not they that carry sorrows know the secret of sorrow. Every heart has a life which it cannot describe nor understand. But naked and open are we before Him with whom we have to do. Thou knowest the thoughts and the intents of the heart. And we pray that thou wilt, in the grace of thy greatness and goodness, vouchsafe to every one in thy presence to-day that which he needs. For emptiness give full supply. For weakness give strength of the right kind in overpowering measure. For sorrow give joy, unless the sorrow be for medicine yet to be taken.

We pray that those who are dim of sight may have vision revealed to them through the Spirit of God. May those that are poor behold what treasures undimmed, and never to pass away, are theirs.

May those that are lonely hear the voice of the church above calling for them in sweet cheer of companionship. May those that are restless and heartsick and homesick be very near to thee and to thy heart, that their hearts may be cured.

We pray that thou wilt grant thy blessing of harmony to all that are in the midst of trouble at home by reason of divided counsels. Bless all that are suffering from the vexations of poverty. Be with all that are perplexed to know the way of duty. To all that do not know how to guide their hand we pray that thou wilt grant that wisdom which is promised from above, and which thou givest liberally, upbraiding not. We pray that parents who are seeking to rear their children aright may know how to touch the sentiments of honor and of truth and of piety in them from the morning of life, and to bring them up to be better than they themselves are.

Bless, we pray thee, all in our midst who are seeking to bring forth a nobler manhood among men, more Christ-likeness, and more power therein. Grant that our schools may live before thee, and be as a garden of the Lord wherein thou dost walk. Wilt thou grant to the teachers and the officers the grace of God and the spirit of the Lord Jesus Christ, that they may bear about in themselves not only the letter of the truth, but also the life of the truth, and be a gospel known and read of all men. We pray for all missions, for all charities, and for all those that administer them. We pray for those that are visiting the sick, and preaching to those who are in prison, and carrying the gospel to those who are in the highways, and seeking to relieve the wants of the world without. As they bear blessings to others, may they receive blessings. And may all of us seek more and more to follow the example and manifest the spirit of Jesus Christ.

We pray for the nations of the earth, that they may learn war no more, and seek the things which make for peace. But if it must needs be that the cup from thy hand shall be drank, if yet it is needful that there should be the chastisements of war, let the bolt descend, let the day hasten, and let the time pass quickly by to bring in that better era afterward in which men shall learn righteousness, and in righteousness learn justice, and love, and dwell together in peace, that all the earth may see thy salvation.

We offer these petitions, not because we are worthy, but in the name of Jesus. For his sake hear us; and to the Father, the Son, and the Spirit shall be praises evermore.

Closing Prayer.

Our Father, we beseech of thee that we may look up and forward into heaven lighted by a Divine Love. May we have a better thought and a nobler measurement of the infinite mercy of God in Christ Jesus. Thou art the God of all the earth. Thou hast proclaimed thyself the Father. Thou hast declared the length and breadth and height and depth of thy love by this—that thou didst die. Thou hast declared that greater love there is not than this. Thou hast made known to us, by all that we can understand, that thy love is the greatest that is conceivable. Into the hands of that love we commit our infant children. Into the hands of that love we give all the members of our household, as one by one they may be taken from us. Into the hands of that love we give the poor, the ignorant, the needy, the perishing, the stumbling ones. Into the hands of that love we give those whose life has been full of blemishes and mistakes. O Lord Jesus Christ, is there not something which thou canst save, and out of which thou canst unfold, in the glory of thy kingdom, the full and perfect stature of holiness? We commend our race to thee. We dare not look at its darkness. We dare not count the years in which the world has rolled in misery. We dare not think of those who have no gospel, no preacher, no church, no institutions of mercy. We dare not think of all those who are cruelly ridden, and worse treated than the beasts of the field. All that we can do is to look up at thee. It will be right in the end. It must be right then. Since thou art a manifestation of God, suffering that others may not suffer, though life be all unexplained and all dark, we have hope in the goodness of God. In our strivings to please thee, and to make attainments in a Christian life, our faith will be that we are to be saved by the grace of God. And if at last we are brought into the heavenly land, we will give praise of our salvation to the Father, the Son, and the Holy Spirit. *Amen.*

Refuge from Trouble.

BEFORE LECTURE-ROOM TALK.

THOU that didst walk upon the water to thy terrified disciples on the sea at night; thou that didst go upon the ship carrying to them peace and gladness, and shame because they feared thee, grant, we beseech of thee, that we may know thee in the night, and upon the swelling sea. When the winds are out, and the storm is cruel, draw near to us, and teach us at last not to be afraid of the coming Christ; for thou hast in thine heart peace enough for thyself, and for all that will trust in thee. Grant to us the power of living above the turmoil of life, and of finding rest in thee.

O Lord our God, may we learn to fly high, as fowls do, that lift themselves up when winter storms come on in the north, and rise higher than the fowler's aim, and make their way into summer and safety far above the reach of danger. Teach us to fly heavenward, high above the earth—too high to be alarmed—so near to thee that always thy hand, lifted, rests upon us, when we cry in the night, even as a mother's hand rests upon the babe in the cradle.

We beseech of thee that thy name may be glorified in that which thou dost to our inward nature; for while we are glad of the bread which comes from thee to nourish our bodies, while we are thankful for thy providence which takes care of us day by day, that which is better than the body —the soul—most needs thy care; and we pray that we may be lifted into that which is pure, and true, and just, and right, and godlike.

O for those thoughts which move in harmony with thine! O for those impulses which, rolling toward the heaven, make no discord among angel choirs! O for that faith which overcomes the world, and discerns through its darkest clouds a bright and eternal gate shining always! O for that soul-rest, for that nesting in the bosom of God, by which we shall be as safe as the sparrow in its nest!

O Lord our God, are not these the things which thou dost desire us to ask? Thou hast granted these things to our fathers, and to our fathers' fathers for many generations. In every age thou hast had thy servants in trouble. They have called to thee from out of dungeons, and from out of exile, and from out of caves of the earth, or when they were wandering to and fro clothed in sheepskins and goatskins—men of whom the world was not worthy; thou hast heard them everywhere; and they are with thee. They are glorified. The world could not hurt them; the fire could not devour them; the axe could not destroy them; the prison could not confine them; nothing could harm them. They have escaped out of every trouble; for ages they have been triumphant; and to them every thought or memory of suffering or fear is as a setting cloud. We are going to follow them. Many of our children have gone on before. Many of our parents are with them in heaven. Many of our nearest friends are there. And how near we are to the pleasure-ground of the universe! How near we are to all whom we have mourned! How near we are to perpetual blessedness among the blessed!

Why should we look upon ourselves as unfortunate, why should we walk as disowned and dishonored paupers, since we are our Father's, under his eye, in his heart, thought of and nourished daily, soon to be crowned, and soon to find the end of sorrow and of burden? O teach us patience, teach us trust, give us a peace which the world cannot take away, give us God; and what need we more!

Thou that wert pierced for us, thou of the wounded side, Jesus, Saviour, we commit ourselves to thee; and in thine arms we are at rest; we commit all our ways to thee, saying, Now glorify thyself! In life or death, in joy or suffering, in honor or dishonor, whatever may be best, mete it out as seemeth best to thee. Give to us only the one gift of faith and trust in thee, and we care not for all the rest.

Wilt thou grant this to all those who are laboring with vulgar cares and sordid sorrows; to all those who are carrying unnecessary burdens and anxieties, and vexing themselves with needless fears; to all those who are in distress for their children or their friends. Teach us the way where we can throw off trouble. Bring us to thee. Why art thou a Saviour, but that we may be saved? If there is an inexhaustible store of love in thee, why should we go without bread, without water, without light and without rest? O thou blessed Saviour, give to thy dear people the secret of making use of thee, that they may walk without care and without burden, and in constant serenity of joy—yea, in songs of triumph.

Closing Prayer.

GRANT unto us, our Father, that we may rise up out of doubt and fear to a higher conception of the grandeur of thine empire, and the clarity of thine heart. May we believe that thy smile pierces the darkness, and that thine eye lights and warms all places where it rests. May we learn, as a bereaved widow, disconsolate, learns, that God is the husband of Time ; and may we believe that all influences are in his hands for gladness through goodness. Help us to review thy way with us, and be ashamed because we have been so unconscious of thy mercies, and because we have let go by such tides of benefaction unrecorded, noting only the salient influences, and allowing to pass unheeded the great procession of thy goodness that incessantly marches by. May we repent that we have been rebellious, and have treated with contempt the pains and pangs that we have felt, but that were messengers of mercy to lift us higher into joy.

Invocation.

VOUCHSAFE to us, O Lord, the token of thy presence, in those gracious affections which spring at thy touch; for we are powerless when we depend upon our own will. Give to us the inward life, the power of discerning thee, the uprising of our secret affection toward thee; and grant that we may draw near to thee with hope, with faith, with love, and with great comfort.

Divine Strength for Human Burdens.

Sunday, January 28, 1877.

THOU ever-blessed God, we rejoice in thee; for though we cannot follow the searching of thine eye, nor by our thoughts follow the flight of thy mind, nor behold the creation in which thou art sitting supreme, God over all, blessed and blessing, yet, with some thoughts and more vague yearnings, we do rise toward thee; we come at least to touch the hem of thy garments, and to rejoice that thou art God, and that there is none beside thee— that there is no divided empire, and no conflict which thou hast not permitted. Thou hast restrained the wrath of man, and caused the remainder thereof to praise thee; and all things go forth in an endless procession of wisdom. That which is dark to us is light to thee, and that which is discordant is coming to harmony in thine ear.

The feeble is growing strong, and the rough places are growing smooth. Thou art bringing down, and thou art exalting. All things shall yet show forth thy glorious goodness and wisdom and nobleness; and then we shall behold thee, not with mortal eyes, blinded by excess of light. When we are transformed into thy likeness, and the soul can see, we shall behold thee; the heart will rejoice in thee with joy unspeakable and full of glory; and there shall be silence in heaven. All hearts will be too full to speak. There will be joy and out-breaking songs there when thou shalt by thy word and by thy look call forth from the souls of those that are saved all tremblings of gladness and all thoughts of ecstasy.

We thank thee that thou art by light as well as by darkness bringing on the seasons, tempering both day and night to the wants of creation. We thank thee that thou art guarding thy people in the winter and in the summer; in the darkness and in the light; through sorrow and through joy. Through suffering the Captain of our salvation was made perfect, and through suffering shall his disciples be made perfect. Yet, for the joy that was set before thee—for the joy that thou didst have even in thy sorrows—thou didst maintain thy purposes, thou didst redeem our souls; by joy in sorrow we would live; and we pray that that grace may be given to us which shall cast upon all the darkness through which we pass the light of thy countenance. Glorious are storm-clouds when the sun shines upon them; and our troubles are made luminous when we know them to be sent of God, and conducted mercifully for our good.

We pray that thou wilt comfort those who are cast down. Inspire hope in those who are despondent, and patience and long-suffering in those that are weary of trouble. Give light to those who are looking in vain toward the east; and say to those who wait and watch, The night is far spent, and the day is at hand.

Grant, we pray thee, that those whose shoulders are weary of their burdens may be able to stand in Another's strength, if not in their own. Give for the crosses which come to us all celestial strength. Thou upon the cross, in weakness and in death, wert mightier than the things that were; and grant that in our weakness, our crosses, we may

DIVINE STRENGTH FOR HUMAN BURDENS. 129

feel the secret power of God in us. We pray that more and more we may be so transformed in our lives that we shall be capable of understanding thee better. We cannot reason to thee. We cannot by searching find thee out. Only by growing unto thee, only by coming into thy likeness, only by partaking of thine experience, can we lift ourselves above the physical things of this life, and come to spiritual light and life and harmony and joy. Vouchsafe, by the power of the Holy Ghost, this transforming influence to every one that wrestles with sorrow; to every one that contests the hard way of life; to every one that seeks to perform duty in the midst of labor and tears and despondency.

We pray thee to bless all the families that are represented in this congregation. Bless the parents, and make them more as gods to their children. Bless the little ones, and grant that they may grow up in the nurture and admonition of the Lord.

Bless all thy servants who go forth in their various fields of labor, and in their several endeavors to bear forth to men the message and the spirit of the Gospel. Grant, we beseech of thee, that every one, at home and everywhere, may breathe that sweetness, that purity, that spirituality, which shall make him seem to men as a son of God.

We pray that thou wilt be pleased to bless our whole land and people. Wilt thou by thy Spirit so temper the hearts of men to equity and to fellowship one with another that no trial, no disturbance, no storm, shall be able to unsettle that peace which God gives.

Closing Prayer.

WE thank thee, our Father, for the lessons which thou hast granted us in thy word. Accept our thanks for the experiences of good men in every age. May we interpret the word of truth by the revelations which thou art making from human life. Teach us to add the unwritten Bible to the Bible record. We pray that thou wilt be on the side of all those who are weak and ready to perish. Raise up in them the power of resisting evil. Inspire in us the disposition to care for those that are unable to care for themselves. Unite us together in the bonds of a common union. Teach us dependence upon the bounty of an ever-loving God. Deliver us from all evil, strengthen us in all good, and bring us, at last, through the unspeakable grace and mercy of our Lord and Saviour Jesus Christ, where we shall be permitted to enter the company of the blessed in the heavenly land.

Invocation.

WHAT are we, that we should mingle our voices, coarse and discordant, with the voices of those that sing everlastingly, with joy and with love, in thy presence, O God! And yet the voice of our children, though they be in the cradle and inarticulate, is sweet, and thou canst hear music where we hear but discord, and thou canst gather pleasure where we can only feel pain. For thou art God. Now, we beseech of thee that thou wilt accept the offerings which we bring to thee—our thoughts, though they droop; our affections, though they be poor; our desires, though they be mistaken. Be pleased, even for thine own sake, to look upon us with great grace, and love, and compassion, this morning, and hear us, and guide us through every step of our services. Bless to us this whole day of rest, that it may be a day in which the heavens shall open above us and cause the earth to smile. So may our Sabbaths, as they succeed each other, be blessed of thee till we enter that rest which remaineth for the people of God.

For Faith in the Unseen.

January 27, 1878.

BEFORE we ask thee, our wants are supplied. It is not by our supplication that the sun comes forth, bringing light and heat. Thy bounty rolls the day and seasons, whether or not thou art questioned or solicited. To all—to the good and the bad, to the just and the unjust—thy ways upon the earth are ways of bounty. Thou art gracious and merciful; restoring, and not slaying. We rejoice in the greatness of thy nature, and we rejoice that the royalty of that nature is in thy goodness. This is beyond anything that we know or can know. What is the height and the depth and the length and the breadth of God's goodness no man may understand. It transcends all human price, and all that we have seen. We shall not find thee diminished when we behold thee as thou art. Thou wilt not be less glorious, but more glorious than we think thee to be. All that the thought can compass, all that the imagination can conceive, and all that the tenderest experience of earth has known, will be thrown into darkness when the splendor of thy nature shall come to be apparent to our cleansed and resurrected souls. We shall rejoice, not in the outward life, nor in ourselves, but in the common possession, with all thy children, of the glory of our God. Then, marshaled, we shall move on, unbroken in rank, built up in knowledge and holy dispositions, and made like unto thee, every one fulfilling some part of that concordant life which is music and gladness.

We look out of the clash of this lower sphere as if heaven were impossible. Yet it remains; that glorious realm exists; and we are drawn near to it. We believe that not many days shall elapse before some of us will stand in Zion and before God, and that all the suffering of this present life will be, as a storm of years gone by, forgotten.

We pray, therefore, that we may beforehand, by apprehension of faith, discern the reality of the invisible life, overcoming the things that are by the things that are not; overcoming actual fatigue, sickness, discouragements, temptations, and the hopelessness of this life, by the power of hope and faith in the life that is to come. May we be mighty through thy Spirit, so that we shall be able, having done all, to stand against all, and be victorious.

We thank thee for the experiences of years past. We thank thee for our chastisements. We thank thee for our mistakes. Yea, we thank thee for those transgressions whose pardon has opened up to us the love and mercy of our God. And we pray, O Lord, since we have learned what thou art by thy mercy toward us, that now love may constrain us, and that in faithfulness to thee we may do no thing that will grieve thee. May we press forward to do the things that please thee. And we pray that thou wilt inspire in us a loftier conception of holiness of life, and more and more spiritual power to attain unto it. We thank thee that there are some who have reached nearly to the borders of that land of settled peace, where the shining of the sun is perpetually upon them; and we beseech of thee that thou wilt cheer others who hunger and thirst after righteousness; and may their aspirations toward it be fulfilled. We pray that more and more of us may be ambitious in spiritual things, and less and less ambitious in things of the outward life—in the pomp and vanities of time. May more of us have a holy and chastened desire for those things which shall bring them into thy favor, and into communion with thee.

We pray that thou wilt comfort any that are for the time obscured—from whom thy face seems hidden. We pray that thou wilt remove the cloud, that they may see thee, and come to thee as children, and that they may no longer dwell in the thraldom of slavery, and under the bondage of fear.

Bless all who are assembled here this morning. May they have come to meet thee; and may they not be disappointed. Reveal thyself as thou knowest how to reveal thyself to every one by name, that he may know that God hath thought of him, and that he hath laid up treasures of mercy for him. And grant to each one, this morning, the intimation of that blessing which he needs of light, of strength, of direction, of confirmation of the presence of thy Spirit.

We pray that thou wilt help all those who are in the relation of parents to be faithful to their covenant vows, to their promises to thee, and to their duties to each other. And grant thy blessing to rest upon the children. May those that are yet young grow up into manhood not soiled nor wounded. May they grow strong in true virtue. And may those that are stepping upon the threshold of life have a nobler ambition than simply worldly success. May they put high their conception of what is becoming in Christian manhood. Strengthen thou those that are in the midst of life and its temptations, that they may fight the good fight, and maintain the holiness that becomes them and blesses the age. And as their infirmities grow upon them, and as one and another intimation is given them of their dissolution, may they rejoice in these tokens of the promised land, and, being ready to depart, wait patiently for the coming of the Lord Jesus Christ.

Bless, we pray thee, all the brethren of this church that are separated in thy providence from us, from whatever cause. If they are detained at home by reason of sickness, may they have the indwelling peace of the presence of God. If they are upon the great deep, command the winds and the waves that they care for them. If they are pilgrims in other lands, lead them as with a cloud, and protect them. And we pray that all this great brotherhood may grow in grace and in the knowledge of the Lord and Saviour Jesus Christ.

Closing Prayer.

OUR Father, wilt thou add thy blessing to the word of instruction. Grant that there may come to those who are struggling with themselves light which shall release them from their thraldom, and enable them to go forward more joyfully serving thee. Give us to perceive how thou desirest us to live. May we serve thee in our daily life by everything that belongs to our being. By our understanding, by our imagination, by our mirthfulness, may we rise up toward thee. May every part of our souls, efflorescent, show forth our love to God. And when we go hence, bring us to that upper life where we shall see thee no longer as in a glass, darkly or partially, but as thou art.

Invocation.

DELIVER us, our Father, from fear. Even though we may be smothered with guilt and apprehension, make known to us how different is greatness in God from the greatness of man, by which power crushes and overshines the poor and the needy. With thee to be great is to be merciful, condescending, and full of all grace, and love, and gentleness. Thy greatness it is that draws us and wins us. Bring near to us the sense of thy glory in thine excellent love. We pray that thou wilt vouchsafe to us that inbreathing Spirit by which all that is dull and dark in us shall be illuminated; by which our weakness shall be made strong; by which our waverings and uncertainties shall be conformed to all strength of Christ Jesus.

Under Chastisement.

Sunday Morning, Feb. 18, 1883.

THOU, O Lord, hast been gracious unto thy people, and therefore we are yet alive. Thou hast by thy providence brought us into thy presence in life and in strength; and we desire to make mention of the goodness of our Lord to us, and to bring our thanksgiving before thee, and with one voice and heart to bless thy holy name. We have seen shadows and darkness as well as light; and nevertheless we have been sustained by thy right-hand; and not only have we come forth into the light, but, looking back, we have occasion to thank thee even more for chastisements than for joys. Thou hast chastened our pride. Thou hast shown us on what slender foundations we stand. Thou hast made our very strength to be as a shadow. Thou hast caused this world to seem small, as it is, and the other life to seem glorious and full of hope, as it is.

O Lord our God, we pray that thou wilt still listen to thine own heart, and not to our cry. Do not answer those of our prayers which we utter foolishly, but out of thy wisdom and out of thy goodness do exceeding abundantly more for us than we can ask or think.

So we pray that we may walk in the way of thy providence, sure that it is the best way, ever trusting thy goodness, always willing to submit our will to thine, every day living as in the sight of our God, every day living as in the presence of the heavenly land, and every day mingling our thoughts and songs and prayers with those of the blessed that surround thy throne.

We thank thee for this day of ministration and

of rest; for its friendships; for its communion; for its incitements; for its consolations; and now wilt thou further grant thy goodness to us in this hour, giving us light and impulse for things that are high and noble? Grant, we pray thee, that the lessons of thy word and the teachings of the sanctuary may so fall upon the open and honest heart that like good seed they shall spring up and bring forth abundant fruit to the honor and glory of thy name.

Have compassion, we beseech of thee, upon those that are in darkness and trouble; upon those that are bound hand and foot. Thou that dost deliver the prisoners, break the doors and the chains that hold them, whatever they may be, within or without; and bring them forth into liberty and light and joy. Grant, we pray thee, that if there be those who sit in the valley and the shadow of death, they may find in thy Word comfort and consolation, and may discern the rising of the sun of a better day.

May those who are taking their last steps toward the other life be strengthened both in body and with a joyful hope of salvation through Jesus Christ.

Be with those that are sick; deal tenderly with them as they lie helpless; and if the earth seems to them dark, wilt thou make it bright by thy presence, O thou divine Comforter.

We pray that those whose hopes are broken in life, whose prosperity is scattered as chaff, may not give themselves up to useless despair, but may gird up their loins, and resist on every side the evil that confronts them; and that having done all they may still stand.

Have, we beseech thee, in thy special compassion, those who wage conflict in our land with strange disasters.* Lord, we pray that the hearts of their fellow-citizens may be opened, that the poor may not perish at their side, but that there may be rescue of those despoiled by raging waters. We beseech of thee that thou wilt remember the unfortunate in other lands, where thou hast also sent forth tokens of chastisement. May the hearts of men be subdued. May they fear God. May they turn from sin. May they seek in righteousness after the better life.

We pray that thy blessing may rest upon all those who are outcast; upon all those that are sin-sick; upon all those for whose souls no man cares. May the Lord raise up those who shall rescue them; may thy Gospel have power to reach the

---

* Floods at the West.

uttermost parts of the earth; may thy kingdom come in all the world; and may thy glory, dawning, shine brighter and brighter unto the perfect day.

Closing Prayer.

GRANT thy blessing, our Father, upon the word of truth. May it be more and more a stimulus to our consciences. Thou that hast given thyself a sacrifice for sin, thou that hast shed thy blood as an atonement for man, thou that hast taken upon thyself the sins of the world, thou that hast been crucified, the just for the unjust, may that spirit which is in thee, and which thou dost manifest to us as the secret of God's nature, be in us. May we, in our limited sphere, according to the measure of our strength, follow the footsteps of the Saviour, and do to others as he has done to us.

Invocation.

O THOU that art in the midst of praise and rejoicing, reach forth thy thought, and by it give to us some joy that shall rise above sorrow, some strength that shall sustain us in all weakness, some light that shall destroy the darkness, some hope that shall be valiant against fear, that we may have peace this day in God. Open thine heart unto us, thou that sendest the sun and the summer. Hast thou exhausted all thy gifts? Hast thou not much more for us on this poor globe? Bring out of our souls all sweet influences for our comfort and for thy joy and glory. This day, out of thine infinite fullness, give us something that shall make us rich. Grant us a sense of thine amplitude, of thy nearness, of thy sympathy, of thy surrounding power and goodness; that we may not seem to ourselves strangers walking alone, nor pilgrims in the wilderness, nor overborne and desolate by reason of the things that are around about us, but that in the Lord we may be strong and full of gladness and hope and faith, that conquer the world.

For Stability of Faith.

Wednesday Evening, Oct. 9, 1878.

How great are the mercies, O Lord our God, which thou hast prepared for all that put their trust in thee! How great are the treasures of the heavens, and how great are the treasures of the earth! Upon that very plain where now harvests are seen in great abundance men have worked through generations in savage life and found no harvest. All around about us thou hast prepared infinite treasures for human wants, whether men know it or not. Thou hast comfort for those that are in affliction, though they be not comforted. Thou hast strength for those that are weak even if they know not how to take that strength. Thou hast all blessings that are needed, and standest ready to be all things to all, and in all. And yet, with bread enough and to spare, with raiment abundant, and with all medicine, how many are there that go hungry, and naked, and sick, and destitute of all things!

We desire, O Lord, that thou wilt, to all thine other mercies, add that gift by which we shall trust in thee—faith that works by love; faith that abides with us; faith that transforms material things, and gives them to us in their spiritual meanings; faith that illumines the world by a light that never sets, that shines brighter than the day, and that clears the night quite out of our experience. This is the portion that thou hast provided for thy people. We beseech of thee, grant us this faith, that shall give us victory over the world and over ourselves; that shall make us valiant in all temptation and in every direction, and bring us off conquerors and more than conquerors through Him that loved us.

O Lord, thou knowest the strife of every heart. Thou knowest who are troubled with pride of reason, and with various prides of life. Thou knowest who contest with obstinacy; who with vanity; who with selfishness in its different forms. Thou knowest who are striving with their affections. Thou knowest the way of each one, and art guiding each according to the nature of the thing that is in him. We rejoice in the thought that this is so. We would not cast out from our faith the belief that thou art continually around about us by thy providence. To do this would be to take the hope out of our life and the strength out of our hands. For what should we be, lifting ourselves up against the currents of life, if left alone? But since thou art the everlasting God, and holdest those that trust in thee, who can disturb them? They cannot be moved nor swept hither and thither.

Now we desire, O God, to have that stability, that rest, that peace which passeth all understanding. We know that we do not deserve it. Our fears rise up and tell us that it is not ours; our conscience sits in solemn judgment upon us because we have violated our duty; the evil one whispers every suggestion of distrust, and on all sides we find influences striving to thrust us from thee, and from our hope in thee. Yet, though these things slay us, we will trust thee. Thou art our God though we are not worthy. Though we are more sinful than we know, though sin is more guilty than we can conceive, though our ingratitude and dishonor are far beyond any measure we have wherewith to measure, yet thou art nevertheless a God of mercy, long-suffering, pardoning iniquity, transgression, and sin, though thou wilt not clear the guilty.

We beseech of thee that thou wilt help us in the clinging of our pride to evil; and may we find that it is not in vain that our life is hid in thine. May we rise up every day as if we were born anew under the trials that we are called to endure. O, that we might not forever trudge with our faces to the earth where there is no vision! O, that we might look up and see how the heavens grow brighter every year! The future is dawning, and the light approaches closer and closer, and waxes more and more brilliant, as we draw near to the throne. Are not these streaks in the East to tell us that the day is at hand? O, that we may look forward to our heritage, and that we may from the certainty of the joy and glory revealed go back with contentment to bear our burdens and perform our duties in life to the very end! From thee, O blessed Saviour, we draw these hopes. We thank thee because thou art what thou art, and hast done for us what thou hast. We desire, O Lord, afresh to consecrate ourselves to thy service, and to live to bless thy name. And when, having passed through the experiences of this mortal life, we are drawing near to our last hours, with crystalline vision may we behold the eternal city, and rejoice before thee and take our departure, leaving to those behind a testimony that the Christ who can sustain in life can sustain in death. And when we shall have tasted death, may we find that it is immortality— that there is no dying to the saint, but only translation. And in thy presence, glorified, sanctified and saved with an everlasting salvation we will give the praise to the Father, the Son, and the Spirit.

Closing Prayer.

GRANT, our Father, that we may be made wiser day by day. May we be led to see our short-sightedness, our heedlessness, our carelessness, all those things in

FOR STABILITY OF FAITH.

which we are at fault. May we be controlled supremely by the great law of life that governs the heavenly host. We pray that we may more and more put on the bond of love—the girdle that holds together all other parts of the celestial raiment. May we walk from day to day seeking the higher and better life, and draw all men with us. May we make the truth of Christ so beautiful in the sight of men that they, seeing our good works, shall glorify our Father which is in heaven. Help us, we beseech of thee, to overcome sin in all its forms. Cure us of its tendencies. Inspire us with noble aspirations. Have compassion upon our weakness, as thou dost teach us to have compassion upon the weakness of others. Lift us up, and bear us through the varying scenes of life. And when we are called to go hence, grant that we may stand as victors before our heavenly Father, redeemed through Jesus Christ our Lord.

Invocation.

O LORD our God, breathe upon us the blessing of the morning. Vouchsafe to us that divine inspiration by which we shall be lifted above the senses, and into the supreme quiet of thy realm, where thou art, and where they are who have been redeemed and been made joyful forever. We belong to thee. We are of the company of those who seek the New Jerusalem. We ask that we may have some earnest of the blessing which we inherit, and toward which we are traveling. Grant that we may have, in the reading of thy Word, in speaking from its truths, in all our offerings of sacred song, and in our communion of prayer, such divine guidance and help as shall lift us up into the very presence and near to the very heart of our God.

The Lesson of Rest.

Sunday Morning, March 28, 1886.

WE thank Thee, O God, that thou dost ride upon the cloud, and govern the storm. All that to us is dark is light to thee. The night shineth as the day. All that which seems to us irregular and ungoverned, is held in thine hand, even as the steed by the rein. From age to age thou dost control the long procession of events, discerning the end from the beginning; and all the wild mixture, all the confusion, all the sorrow and the suffering, is discerned of thee. As is the palette to the color, as is violence to development in strength, as is the crushing of the grape to the wine, so in thy sight all things are beneficent that to us are most confusing and seemingly conflicting and threatening. Sorrow and pain and disaster are woven in the loom of God; and in the end we, too, shall be permitted to discern the fair pattern, and understand how that which brought tears here shall bring righteousness there.

O, how good it is to trust thee, and to believe that thou art wise, and that thou art full of compassion, as thou carriest on thy great work of love and benevolence, sympathizing with all that suffer on the way, and gathering them at last with an exceeding great salvation! We trust thee, not because we understand thee, but because in many things thou hast taught us where we should have been afraid to trust. We have crossed many a gulf and many a roaring stream upon the bridge of faith, and have exulted to find ourselves safe landed, and have learned to trust thee, as a child a parent, as a passenger the master of a ship, not because we know, but because thou knowest.

We are not called to settle the troubles of to-day

or of to-morrow; we rest in God; and when everything is stripped by the frosts of adversity, when the fold is cut off, when the fig-tree bears no fruit, we yet rejoice in the Lord. And how great is the orb of that joy which is in the Lord, and is the fountain of all other joys! For we are strong in thee, we are light in thee, and we are safe in thee. We rejoice, therefore, that we may put our trust in thee, and cast our burdens upon thee, knowing that thou dost care for us.

Teach us this lesson of rest in our own spirits; and, while we are stirred to activity and to energy, let us not fall into the conceit of supposing that we ourselves work out our own prosperity; for thou, O God, art lengthening our life, impleting our brains, cleansing our hands, and ministering, through thy law, on every side, to all our indifference and thoughtlessness. That which we may not wisely and successfully do is done in the Lord; and if thy thought, which is universal law, were taken away for one moment, we should dissolve and perish. Grant, therefore, that we may be humble in thy presence, and walk softly before God, and yet boldly. In every time of need may we know how to come to thee; and may the way be fragrant where our feet should tread, with thought, and communion, and love, and prayer.

Grant thy blessing upon thy people, this morning, assembled here. Though their lips be silent, what clouds of incense from every heart go up in petitions to thee! Thou knowest, better than they know, both what they need and what they want. We beseech of thee, therefore, that thou wouldst do unto them according to that which is best in thy sight. Grant that they may be clothed with thyself, with thy patience, with thy gentleness, with thy long-suffering, with thy tender mercies, with thy loving-kindnesses. We pray that thou wouldst grant to all of them sympathy with each other, so that they may sing rather than quarrel along the royal road, and rejoice in each other's welfare, the strong bearing with the weak, the wise with the ignorant, and all men recognizing the sanctity of those about them, in that they are of God, and are returning again to God.

We pray for thy blessing to rest upon our whole land ; and in this day of confusion, grant, we pray thee, that more than ever before we may discern the divine hand and the overruling providence, bringing peace out of confusion and advancement out of threatenings. And may thy kingdom come in all the world.

This, indeed, is a year of the revelation of the right-hand of Almighty God. Afar off, the garments rolled in blood tell of war, and the murmuring of the nations of distrust and distress; but there is peace above; thou wilt rain down righteousness to give peace below; all kingdoms shall learn to serve thee; and the unity and brotherhood of mankind shall be secured. While labor-pains are on the earth, when the new man is to be born, let us not, O God, be afraid for crying nor for tears, but may we rejoice in the birth of this man-child.

We commit to thine hand ourselves and all that interests us in time, and all that interests us in the eternities. Lord, we are traveling home. Let not the watchman sleep at the gate when we come to knock. Give us an exceeding and abundant entrance into the kingdom of thy glory. And we will give the praise of our salvation to the Father, the Son, and the Spirit.

Closing Prayer.

OUR Father, we pray that thou wilt teach us the hidden things. We know the way outwardly of right and duty, but our outward life is full of imperfection. The body, being relative to time, needs but little for its carriage across the earthly sphere ; but for the soul, that is to take a nobler flight, wrapped in the garments

THE LESSON OF REST.

of immortality, thou blessed God, thy bosom is needful. Then put forth thine arms, and lift us up, eternal Spirit, and give us a taste of that peace which passeth all understanding. May we learn to live in thee; and, having that life which is hidden with Christ in God, may we rejoice that when He shall appear we shall appear with him, no longer disfigured, but in full majesty, and beauty and power. For the hope of this, and for every step of experience toward it, we render thee thanks. O thou Saviour, we love thee! As the thought of thy nature comes forth to us, our souls rise up to greet thee. Thou art our King because thou art Love. We submit ourselves to thee, saying, Thy will be done—not ours—*Thine.* Receive our dedication. Accept our aspiration —our longing for a nobler life. And take us home when the body shall drop and the spiritual life shall open, that we may in thee find immortality and glory.

Invocation.

THOU, God, infinite in fullness of love and mercy and all helpfulness, look graciously upon us. We are less in thy sight than are the humblest flowers, that lift themselves up, this morning, under the sun. As compared with the greatness of its warmth and life what are they! And what is our littleness before thee! Thou hast brought us forth, O Lord our God, in our helplessness; and thou art standing above and over against all want and littleness with infinite supply. We come, not to thy fear nor to thy wrath, but to thy goodness and to thy mercy; and we say, Our Father, look compassionately and in love upon us, and give us, this day, the bread that we need, as for the body so for the soul. And lead us out of all ways of sin and temptation up into the way where thou art, that we may be able to say, Hallowed be thy name, and rejoice in thee, and find all other joys heightened by this supreme joy. Grant this blessing, to the hour, to the day, and to the year, until this life mingles with the higher, when we will praise thee with voice and thoughts and affections not permitted to the earth.

Lowliness and Royalty.

Sunday Morning, Nov. 7, 1886.

THOU dost accept each servant, dear Lord. Thine heart is as a gate, ever open, and all the royalty of thy kingdom is for these, the humblest and the poorest, to draw them near to thee by faith and by love. Make the experience and the service of to-day blessed in the memory and the whole life of thy servants; and while we are in humble relations on earth, how great is the glory of that invisible kingdom that overhangs us all! How great is that service of love which for evermore undyingly goes on in the invisible realm! Thither our thoughts wander; there we gather strange experiences; we search for our lost ones; we walk with the holy men of old; we rejoice in the joy of that great kingdom of love and music; and yet how faint is our conception, and how far does the lowest and the least in the heavenly kingdom outrun our highest thought and imagination! Blessed be thy name, there remaineth a rest for the people of God. Tempests may blow upon the earth, and kingdoms may rise and fall, and wars may clash and desolate the earth, and all things may change in perpetual revolution or rebound; but there remaineth a rest upon which shall come no storm, which shall not be upset by revolution, nor changed except from glory to glory. To that great rest we aspire. From the weary conflict with ourselves, from our bondage to the flesh, from the thrall of weariness, from the burden of sinfulness, from all sorrow and all that brings trouble, we turn to that blessedness which rests in thy presence.

O Eternal Love, thou art thinking of us to-day, and art drawing us; and this is the meaning of that influence that is calling out to thee, Father, Father! We are children that know not how to requite thy parentage; nor do we do that which we understand; but thou, with eternal love, unsearchable and incomprehensible, art drawing us to thyself. We thank thee that our strength is thy strength, and that our weakness is upheld and filled full of conquest by the victorious power of Him who loved us, and gave himself for us, and who is to make us kings and priests immortal.

We thank thee that we have come home to thy house this morning, and we thank thee for all greetings, for all deep-seated joys, for all hopes, all affections, and all purposes of zeal in thy cause in the days that are to come. Grant, we pray thee, that there may be to-day, not merely an outward manifestation, but a manifestation of those deeper purposes that are in us of a better life, of holier service and of more earnest devotion to the cause of our King.

Bless, we beseech of thee, this Church. Bless all the members of the congregation—all the households that are here represented with us. Remember those that cannot be with us to-day, and that yet are homesick for us; and in their loneliness, or upon their beds of sickness, or in their strifes with misfortune in life, Lord, send to them, to-day, some indication that they are remembered, and that the sanctuary hath also a gift for them. And be with all those, we beseech of thee, that are in trouble to-day, by reason of the sorrows and bereavements that have fallen upon them. O, thou that lovest them, reveal in their sorrow the divine life; and may they not question thee, but only seek to know what thou wouldst have of them, to be justified, that they may live purer and nobler lives. Bring to us, to aid every one of us, a higher standard of thought and duty, and simpler determinations to lift up our banner, and to march higher and nobler than before.

Remember the dear children in all our schools— the army of those that are coming on; and may their feet take hold upon Zion.

We beseech of thee, grant thy blessing to those that are wistfully looking upon the outward forms of life and religion. Bring them into the interior of Christian life—the experience of the spirit and love of God, and the soul's consecration of Jesus Christ. O, make this a fruitful year. May we sow liberally, that we may reap abundantly, and may thy name be glorified in our midst.

Lord, look not upon us alone. In the great thrall, in the wild excitements that fill our day, O, be thou the Guide of the storm, and direct all things for the furtherance of thy glory. Look upon the nations far abroad. Be gracious unto them, and suffer not tyranny nor violence nor rude revolution to prevail in the world. More and more may thy hand of righteousness be discerned in the affairs of men.

And now, Lord, we ask for higher inspiration, for more courage, for more strength, for more sympathy with thee in well-doing, that thy name, and not ours, may be glorious in the sight of the people. We pray for thy kingdom, that it may come through the ages long delayed, and that the glory of the Lord, at last, may rise upon the earth, the unsetting sun that shall shine with blessings for a thousand years.

Closing Prayer.

GRANT Thy blessing, our Father, to rest upon thy truth, and upon our knowledge of it. Behold our weakness, our trembling feet, our feeble hand, our faith that needs every day to be re-illumined, our love that wants kindling anew every day, and in thine infinite compassion pour out thy life upon us. We can receive thee, not in the flesh, but only in the spirit. Grant, therefore, that we may so live by faith as to be evermore conscious of the movements of God around about us and within us, and that we may triumph over the physical man—over all memory of the past—over its sins and mistakes. May we not stumble at dead things which long ago should have been buried. May we revive that earnestness, that zeal, that noble purpose, that holy aspiration, that higher conception of our final estate of manhood in heaven, which inspires us in our best moments. Let us look away from things beneath and backward, and let us look upward and onward, that our thought may move toward the heavenly land ere we go forth, as on angels' wings, with joy, to meet thee and dwell with thee forever

Invocation.

LOOK forth upon our darkness, O thou Morning of light and of love. There is no darkness nor any night with thee. In a settled and eternal gladness they dwell who behold thee and are like unto thee. We, too, are heirs expectant, waiting. Breathe forth upon us some sense of our relationship to thee, and of our treasure in thee. Look upon our low estate and nature, and make haste to help us, that our evil tendencies may perish, that our upward aspirations may gain fullness of strength, that above all fear, doubt, worldliness, and sordid care, we may rise and soar heavenward upon the pinions of joy and faith. We pray that thou wilt bless all the instrumentalities we employ for edification, for instruction, for fellowship and rejoicing; and may all things, this day, be honorable in thy sight and blessed in our using.

The Vitality of Goodness.

WE have found it good to draw near to thee, our Father, not as suppliants, nor as beggars: for our great and abiding wants are provided for by the continual presence of thy messengers; and day by day the light and the darkness are administered to us; and day by day the fruit of summer is borne to us; and thou, that carest for the birds and for the beasts, yet more abundantly dost care for us. We rejoice in the constancy and the universality of thy providence; but we are not content to be happy in the body and in our outward estate alone. We need thee. We need a sense of thy power and wisdom and presence. We need to believe that the everlasting Being who presides over all human affairs is pure, is just, and is full of love and kindness. We need to know, and to have brought home to us as from the very atmosphere, that thou hatest the things that are harmful, and dost rejoice in the things that are beneficial, and art discriminating between the good and the evil, between the just and the unjust; and that it is established forever that the things which work for pain and for sorrow shall perish when their ministration is over, and the things which work for good are everlasting. The name of the wicked shall rot, but the righteous shall be held in everlasting remembrance; sighing and groans shall cease, but the voice of joy shall never cease; and all corruptions, yea and death itself, shall die, but love, mounting to higher spheres, shall go on forever. This is thy government. These are the courses which thou dost hold, and into which thou art convoking universal affairs; and we need to have a sense of thy supereminent providence, of thy personal presence, and of thy disposition, which is toward righteousness, with all joy and gladness. The sight of our eyes vexes our hearts; and we behold daily how goodness is supplanted, how evil runs riot, and how corruption triumphs on every side; and we need something for the sense, something for our faith. In thee we have all things; and we rejoice, even when we can rejoice in nothing else, in the Lord. We trust in the Lord when our sight fails; and in the Lord we are strong; and in thee we shall triumph: not by our own might, nor by our own wisdom, nor by our own goodness, but by the generous love of Him that loved us even unto death, that we might come off conquerors and more than conquerors.

We pray that this truth may be brought home to us sinners in need, that in times of temptation we may be able to cover ourselves with it as with a garment, yea, and wear it as a shield and an armor. And may we be able to run unto thee as into a fortress; and may we hide in thy pavilion till the storm be overpast. So be thou a God not far off, but near at hand; may we behold thy presence in every time of need; and may our hope in thee be built, not alone on other men's testimony, but on thine indwelling power, in thine affection, and in thy love.

We pray that thou wilt break down whatever middle wall of partition there is. Destroy whatever darkness-breeding thing there is, by the light of the glory of God as it shines in the face of Jesus Christ. May thy children escape out of harm. If their sins rise up between thee and them, overcome, we pray thee, all powers that hold them in thrall to sin. If it be doubt, if it be want of faith, that has them in bondage, minister to them, we pray thee, in thy gracious providence, that which shall enable them to comprehend thee, and be filled with a sense of thy Being, and of the blessedness of thy presence.

We pray for all those who have wandered away from thee, and who remember days of love and of joy, but who remember them as things that shall be seen no more. O Lord, we pray that thou wilt draw near to all those who have backslidden, to all those whose love and zeal are quenched, and to all those who have wandered into ways of unbelief by forsaking the ways of their fathers. May they return to thee and to thy fold.

Keep, by thine own power, we beseech of thee, those who have not yet fallen. Grant that they may more and more stand firm in the Lord against fear, against every blandishment, against all abhorrent evil.

And we pray that thy power may be in the midst of this congregation. Revive thy work in the hearts of thy people here. Grant, we pray thee, that the spirit of prayer may break forth and flow as mighty streams flow. May the young be filled with the love of God, and with that fear of God which is the beginning of wisdom. Wilt thou bless all that labor in our midst—the teachers and officers of our Sunday-schools, and of our Bible classes, and of our missions, and of the merciful institutions which thou hast inspired thy people to erect. Grant that all of them may be clothed with the purity and the sweetness and the gentleness of the Lord Jesus Christ, that they may themselves be burning and shining lights in the midst of darkness and trouble.

We pray for thy churches. We thank thee that thou art drawing them nearer together, and that thou art breaking down more and more repellent prejudices, and bringing into confidence all men who are laboring for the same sweet end. May this blessed work go on, and may nothing hinder it till all thy people shall be as one—one in the communion of the Lord; one in faith; one in zeal; one in affection; one in self-sacrificing labor. And we pray for those who are laboring on the outskirts of civilization, in the weak and destitute places of our own land. Bless those who are preaching and teaching among the enslaved, or those who have just been emancipated from slavery, and in the isles of the sea, and in the dark places of the earth, bearing the knowledge of the Saviour. O Lord, give them courage, give them patience, give them faith, that when the sight refuses to cheer and to encourage them they still may be able to endure, by reason of things unseen, the invisible realities.

Closing Prayer.

LORD, have compassion upon our blindness. We, too, sit by the wayside, and, hearing that thou art passing, call out to thee, Lord, have mercy! And if rebuked, with yet more zeal and earnestness we cry, Thou Son of David, have mercy upon us! We know that thou dost hear us, ask what we will; and we pray that thou wilt remove this blindness. Give us second-sight. Make us to see things beyond this mortal sphere. May we dwell with a perpetual consciousness of eternal life. Enable us to fix our thoughts on thee and thy truths from day to day and from hour to hour. Help us to overcome ourselves, and to manifest in our lives the beauty of new men in Christ Jesus. May the services of the sanctuary this day be blessed to every one of us. Be with us through the week. May we rise into the consciousness, the security, and the joy of being with thee. And be with us in our worldly affairs. Deliver us from bondage to the flesh. And when our career on earth is ended, while men weep may angels rejoice; while men say, They are gone, may the great host say, They have come; and while men say, They are dead, say thou, Enter into eternal life.

Invocation.

GRANT to us something of that joy which they have, our Father, who are redeemed from the trouble of this life, and who stand before thee kings and priests unto God. For though we are not yet out from under the yoke and the burden, we are the sons of God. Of us thou art thinking. For us thy heart is warm. Over us the Hand that guides the universe is extended. There is light to break through the darkness, and the joy that comes from the morning to overcome the sorrow of all the world. Give to us, this morning, some realization of the infinite blessedness of the world that is to come, and make us patient in bearing all the discipline and whatever is needful to cleanse us from the flesh, and bring us unto the Spirit as sons of God.

Grant thy blessing, this morning, in every service—in singing; in reading thy Word; in all the offices of devotion; in instruction · in meditation; in inspiration. And may thy name be honored in the enlarging of our souls, through Jesus Christ our Redeemer.

The Better Land.

November 21, 1886.

OUR Father, our heart's desire is toward thee, toward our home, this morning. Behold, how we wander and are lost! See, how unwearied are selfishness and pride, that perpetually lie in wait for us; how in alternation with that which is best in us they rise up with earnest endeavor, and how to do good is not present with us. Behold what struggle, what slow attainment, what retrogression there is, and have compassion upon us; for we are very weak: strong in desire, but feeble in the fulfillment thereof.

There is a land of the blessed where no sun shall rise, for days are not measured there; nor is there any moon there to give light by night. Thou art the light thereof; and all that are gathered therein have eternal joy and eternal peace—joy that leaves no regrets behind, and peace that chides not. We do not know, we cannot conceive, what that life must be in which the body is dropped, and the processions of this world have passed away and only the spirit is left. We do not understand its law, nor its experience, nor anything of it, save that we shall be as thou art, that thy glory shall be our light, and that thou art the cause of that joy which shall forever and forever abide, and fill the cups that never empty.

We rejoice that that great estate is so near to us. Thou dost not reserve it always till men have toiled through many, many years. Thou dost lead into it the little ones that have had no experience of earth and sin. Thou callest saints from the cradle. Thou takest those that are yet children, those that from the beginning of their years walk in an inexperienced life, those from out of the burdens and the midst of life itself, and those that are ripe and strong. Thou hast not filled up, blessed be thy name, the whole realm; and yet thou hast filled the seats that waited for multitudes whom we have known and loved. Their life is with us in memory. They do not forget us. They love us better than when they were on earth; and we are hastening thither to meet them again, where all care shall have departed forever.

Grant that, in the hope and certainty of this rest which remaineth for the people of God, we may lift up our head in the midst of storm, undiscouraged and undismayed. May we walk worthy of the high vocation wherewith we are called. May we not, with coward hearts, turn into complaint our experience from day to day, but bear hardness as good soldiers. May we not be made haughty by worldly prosperity, nor be depressed by adversity. May we take all things as sent of God. May all experiences, all joys, all sorrows, be as so many schoolmasters, training us for the higher life. Grant that we may walk with an even mind from day to day, full of hope and full of the joy that is to come.

Grant a blessing to rest, we pray thee, upon all that are troubled this morning. As thou didst, in the twilight hour, stand in the midst of thy disciples, and spread thy hands towards them, and say, Peace be with you, so stand in this congregation, this morning, and say to every one, Peace, from God, be with you. Grant that the light may fall upon those that sit in darkness. Grant that strength may come to those who are of a weak heart and a feeble faith. May the lame walk here today, and the lepers be cleansed. Grant that they who are wanderers may find themselves coming back from the swineherd and from their far-away wanderings to their loving and waiting Father. May this be to them a day of illumination, of hope, of joy, and of peace that passeth all understanding.

Dwell in every household that is represented here. Be the God of the little children. Thou thyself that didst walk the ways of childhood, have compassion upon our children and our children's children.

Be with all those that are in perplexity and doubt in regard to their happiness. May they know how to cast their burden on the Lord, who careth for them.

Grant, we pray thee, that those who are bereaved and who sit in the memory of their great sorrow may find companionship in thee, thou that hast been the Consoler of ages. While thou knowest thy work, we know it not. Thou canst comfort them, for thou art the God of all consolation. We pray that thou wilt help those who see men as trees walking—who discern truths only as mystery figured before their minds. Grant that in all the truths that pertain to our salvation we may have that lens of love through which all things are plain. Teach us to discern thy nature, and the nature that thou wouldst have in us. In our pilgrimage may we not wander from the great highway of the Lord.

We pray for all the peoples of the earth, and especially for all those that are put under our care, or upon whom our examples are falling. Remember the labors of thy servants, the missionaries among our own native tribes, among those that are liberated,—the children of Africa,—among all the scattered ones up and down throughout this land, speaking many tongues, but all of one household, all children of God. Grant that they who labor under great discouragements may gird up their loins from day to day and from week to week, with courage given them from on high, knowing that they shall reap if they faint not.

Closing Prayer.

Our Father, grant that the word spoken may bring forth in us fruit unto everlasting life; and bringing forth fruit, may we also by our example and influence lead others to fruitfulness. Wilt thou bless us when we sing once more; wilt thou go with us to our homes; and when life itself is over wilt thou bring us to that better household and nobler parentage above, whence we shall go out no more forever.

Invocation.

BE pleased, O God, to give forth from thine infinite fullness a supply for our want. Day by day we feed upon thee; and yet the loaf is not wasted. The light is not consumed that hath streamed for ages; and we rejoice that the light and warmth of thy nature hath supplied our fathers, supplies us, and shall supply us forever. Now we pray for thy presence, which we may know by the lifting up of all joy and hope and trust. By faith we shall discern the invisible things of life in our better nature. So make manifest thyself to us that we shall feel that which is best of us arise toward thee, and calling after thee, that we may become indeed the sons of God. Accept the service that we offer to thee. Accept and bless all our endeavors at edification, at worshiping, at rejoicing in the Lord; and here, in the sanctuary, at our homes, by the way, everywhere, may this be a day of thankfulness to thee, and of rest and joy in thee.

From Generation to Generation.

Thanksgiving Day.

LORD GOD of our fathers, we draw near to thee, rejoicing in the mercies which thou hast granted unto us, both in the days gone by, and in the days at hand through which we are passing. We thank thee that we have had the pious example of those who went before, their love unfeigned, their reverence for thee and for thine ordinances, their love for their fellow-men, and their willingness to sacrifice themselves for the sake of those who should come after. We thank thee that by the inspiration of thy Spirit through thy Word thou didst guide our fathers to the founding of wise institutions, to the establishment of goodly laws, and to the procedure which has set an example to the ages, of virtue in administration. We rejoice in all that wide-flowing beneficence which hath followed their management of public affairs. Thou hast made a city of the wilderness. Thou hast covered this land with people. Where before there were none to know and recognize the glory of thy power on every side, now towns and villages pour forth praise unto God.

We thank thee for the mercies which have gone on from generation to generation, dispersing darkness, overcoming obstacles, finding a way when men were baffled, and still, by thy providence made manifest in the sight of men, opening before the feet of those who went before, a large place. Though we have stumbled and fallen into many transgressions, and though we have received at thine hand punishment for our sins, in the midst of thy wrath thou didst remember mercy, and thou hast brought us forth out of confusion, and peril, and death, and hast established our goings in the way of peace, and hast held together this mighty nation which only the omnipotent power of God could have welded; and thou art leading us forth yet through some trial and some tribulation, and art giving us strength to bear, so that with every trouble comes divine wisdom and divine succor.

We thank thee for all the unbounded and immeasurable prosperity of the field and the sea. We thank thee for all that peace which thou hast granted us among ourselves; for concord; for thriving industries; for the amassing of substance and wealth; for the founding of institutions; for the prevalence of law; for the going forth of the light of knowledge; for the education of the ignorant and the outcast. We thank thee for courts, for magistrates, for judges, and for the administration of law by which violence is suppressed among this great people.

And underlying all this, O Lord our God, we thank thee that thou hast built up churches in our midst, and that thou hast poured out thy Spirit upon one and another, and upon multitudes, and that thy Word has gone forth with freedom to and fro in this land where thou hast established liberty, and that multitudes have been brought personally to the Lord Jesus Christ as their Saviour while his spirit and influence have had power in our nation.

Lord God of our salvation, Lord God of this nation, Lord God of our fathers, we commend ourselves to thy care now, asking that wisdom may be sent down from above; and we commend ourselves to thee in the future. Thou that didst open the way out of Egypt through the sea and through the desert and across the river—has thine hand forgot leadership? Still lead this people: yet not through the Red Sea, if it be thy pleasure, but through ways of peace, that we may forget the sight of blood, and hear the cry of suffering no more. And we beseech of thee that thou wilt still put it into the hearts of thy people to dwell together in concord. Spread abroad the light of intelligence by wise institutions, that this land from side to side may be filled with knowledge and virtue and true piety.

Closing Prayer.

OUR heavenly Father, wilt thou grant thy blessing to rest upon the word which has been spoken. Not only may we have an intellectual interest in it, but may it become experimental with us. Hold us back from evils. May we not be of those who measure themselves among themselves, and compare themselves with themselves, and are not wise; may we be of those who say, Search me, O God, try thou me, and see if there be any evil way in me. So search us, so humble us, so discipline us in every part of our lives, that at last we may be followers of Christ, acknowledged by him.

Invocation.

THOU that never slumberest nor sleepest, Watchman of Israel, thou that hast brought us out of feebleness and the darkness of the night again to light, to consciousness, and to hope, thou art the Source of our life; and we come to thee this morning. Since thou hast granted us the life of the body, and the clearness of understanding, grant us that other and better light of the Spirit, by which we shall discern, as if by the senses, the invisibility of thy kingdom. Especially draw near to us that we may have some sense of relationship with thee, and that we may feel what glory there is in thee, and that it is ours; what power and wisdom and providence, and that they are ours, because we are Christ's. And we pray not only that thou wilt grant this reviving influence, but that every endeavor which we shall make under its stimulus may be divinely inspired and guided and blest—the reading of thy Word, the fellowship of song, the communion of prayer, meditation, and rejoicing in fellowship with each other.

The Communion of Saints.*

WE rejoice, our Father, that there is an airy road which mortal feet can never tread, but which is

* Immediately following the reception of members into the church.

familiar to those that are in the spirit-land. We thank thee that the distance between them and us is not great. Though we cannot by our bodily organs discern the way to the great life that is beyond, nor understand how it is that they who are so silent, and so separate from us, should yet be near to us, and should fulfill the functions of love toward us, thou understandest it, and that is enough. Since it is thy good pleasure that the veil should be dropped between our seeing and the things seen, we will wait till thine hand shall lift it or bear us through. It hath not entered into the heart of man to conceive the things which thou hast laid up for us. Something has been interpreted to us by the Spirit here; but more remains uninterpreted. The height, the depth, the length, and the breadth of the love of God as manifested through Jesus Christ cannot be known by these narrow and selfish hearts of ours. It passes understanding. But there is a heaven made by thy love, there is a realm of joy unbounded by human thought, and unspeakable by human language; and into that state of blessedness have entered, how many! How many that have been near to us! How many that taught us! How many at whose knees we first called thee Father! How many that endeared life to us, and made it darker when they left! They have accomplished their warfare, their conflict is over, and they rest. Yet they are not insensible to our warfare and our conflict, which they witness with a consciousness of reality that we lack, and with a perpetual zeal which we have not.

We rejoice that there is the ministry and the communion of the saints, and that we have the sympathy of that great cloud of witnesses who throng the horizon, and look upon the level of the life which we tread to see whether we carry ourselves worthily. And if they could speak again in human language, as once they spoke, what sweet words of encouragement would they breathe to us, urging us to be patient until the end, trusting in God! O how boundless must be God's greatness to those who are perfected so that they can see it! How strange to them must seem the unbelief in which they dwelt when they were on earth, and our unbelief who stand without the orb shivering in the winter of time without faith! How strange must seem our low estate to them, who glow and rejoice with joy unspeakable and full of glory!

We pray that thou wilt lift up our thoughts this morning, that, broken-winged, lie upon the ground, or that crawl when they should fly. Intone our voices this morning, that instead of speaking in sighs, and with tears, we may speak with joy and rejoicing. Give to us a transmuting power by which we may see things not as what they are to the outward sense; by which we may know the finer meanings of life; by which we may see the channel in which all these lower and grosser things do move; and grant to us a realization of thine own presence, and of our relationship to thee. May there be something in our souls to-day that shall clasp thee, and not let thee go. May we be able to say with all the fervor of love, Thou art ours! Thou dost belong to us because we belong to thee, merciful Saviour. Thou that hast sought us, and hast found us, and hast spoken to us some words of love, we hold thee to thy words. Thou shalt not leave us. We will not go alone. We are thy children. We are beloved of thee. For us thou hast suffered. For us thy blood has been shed. We have nothing of our own to plead, but we plead thee. And thou canst not be untrue nor unfaithful. Thou art our shield; our staff; the food of our daily life; the bright star of our hope; our rising sun, and our day. Our life is hid in thine, and thou canst not cast us away. We cling to thee. We will not let thee go—even if thou wouldst we would not; but thou wouldst not! When all others forsake thine own, then thou searchest them out, and speakest comfortable words unto them. Though thou seemest sometimes, by our reckoning of time, to wait long, there is no long waiting to thee. Thou wilt avenge thine elect, and speedily it shall seem to them when they judge as thou judgest.

Now we beseech of thee, O Lord Jesus, that thou wilt draw near to all those who have borne thy name, and who have sought to bear thy spirit also. Grant, we beseech of thee, that their imperfection, their ignorance, their variableness, their actions and retroactions, may not be numbered against them. And yet may they never forget thee. May all the souls in thy presence who have been redeemed by thee, and who are living by faith in thee, bear in mind their deficiency, mourn over their sinfulness, hate the evil that is in them, lift themselves to a larger thought of the obligation of honor and love, and learn more and more to live by the power of the unseen and the unknown.

We pray that thy blessing may rest especially upon thy servants who have come among us today, and who by their public act have visibly united themselves to us. Be very gracious unto them, comfort them with the consolations of the Holy Ghost, and sustain them in all their pilgrimage here below, that they may walk in the way of their fathers, and have the blessings of their fathers' God resting upon them abundantly.

Be near to all that are in trouble; and may they be consciously near to thee. Open the way to those who are perplexed. Lift the burdens from shoulders that cannot bear them any longer, or put thine own everlasting strength beneath them and hold them up.

Grant, we pray thee, that those who are bereaved, and whose hearts have been deeply pierced, may have the sustaining grace of God. Thy grace can sustain us even in emergency. There is nothing that can destroy those that trust thee. Thou canst lift them up and enable them by faith to overcome visible things in this life; and thou canst give them victory in death. We pray that thou wilt sustain the weak, and the poor, and the tempted, and the wandering, and all that need thee. Manifest thyself by the abundance of thy mercy and thy pity among thy people.

Closing Prayer.

OUR Father, we beseech of thee that thou wilt grant thy blessing to rest upon us in the reading of thy Word. We rejoice that thou hast given us a record of thy dealings of old; that thou hast uttered thy thoughts and feelings; that thou hast made known thy will; that thou hast filled this thy book full of all sweet messages; and that therein we are not threatened but persuaded and encouraged. We thank thee for the munificence of all that by means of it thou hast vouchsafed to us for our education in spiritual things. We love to think that it is the book which our fathers read, that we are reading the lines that comforted our mother, and that our brothers and sisters who have gone home went on the strength of the Bible by which we are seeking to strengthen ourselves. As thy saints in times past have been victorious in overcoming the world through the strength they received from the teaching of this Word, so we pray that thou wilt enable us, through the instruction which we may derive from that book also to overcome the world, and join with the host of thy faithful ones.

We are grateful for the experiences we have already had in its use day by day; and we desire to avail ourselves of its benefits more and more. And grant that we may be delivered from all vanity, from all combativeness, from all hatefulness toward other persons, in using it. May we accept it as thy blessed Word to us. May we wrap ourselves in it as in a garment. May we feed ourselves upon it as upon a loaf. May it be to us as a fountain, that we may drink of its refreshing waters. As a lamp may it light our path. May we heed its precepts till we no more need its ministrations.

Then may the day break that shall know no setting of the sun—the day without a sun; and may we enter that land that is without temple, on whose shore beats no wave, and on whose sky comes no storm, and where God is the light, the joy, and the peace. And to thy name shall be the praise of our salvation, Father, Son, and Spirit.

Invocation.

FORTH from out of thine infinite fullness, O thou whose thoughts move the endless procession of summer in all fruitfulness and beauty, forth from thine own self, the Center of excellence, give to us, this day, life and light and joy, that we may seem to ourselves to be enwrapped by our God, to live in him, to partake of him, and to be apprehended by him. Remove all doubts, all darkness, all misapprehension from our minds; and as thou dost blow away the clouds and storms, that we may behold the stars by night and the sun by day, so may our fear and care be driven away, that this morning we may behold thee, and rejoice in thee, feel thy life and find warmth in thee. This is our privilege and thy gift. Behold our weakness, and help us to such strength as is needed. May all holy thoughts go forth ascending; and before thee may our poor sacrifice—the best that we can offer, and yet poor—be acceptable to thee, not for its sake, but for the sake of the love which thou bearest toward us, thy children, and for thine own name's sake.

For a Restoration of Faith.

OPEN our understanding, O God, that we may discern thee. Deliver us from the thrall of our senses; and, that we may not trust them in over-measure, nor be mastered or guided by them, deliver us from the thought that thou art to be found in agents of power, or that the things which come to the eye, or fill it with wonder, represent thee. Deliver us from thinking that only in government, in industry, and in the great world of society there is thy power; grant unto us to appreciate the silence of God, thy gentleness, thy meekness, the unrevealed mystery of thy presence. Give us an inward light to discern, an inward hearing, that we may gather what thou hast to say to thy silent ones. O, give us soul-power. Give us that power of faith by which to discern unimaginable things, and lift us into those altitudes of the soul where we shall meet thee, where thy thoughts are powerful, and where every being distills influence.

Deliver us, we beseech of thee, from all those misconceptions and overestimates of human life that turn upon the life that now is—upon our bodily condition. For we belong to heaven, we belong to our Father's household, but we have lost our way back thither, and we grope, we stumble, we grieve in discouragements, or we sit down in contentment with the things which we find by the way, willing to be exiled—perpetually exiled.

Now, grant unto us, we pray thee, the lost

hunger and thirst after righteousness—the longing for God. Grant unto us that drawing power by which everything that is in us shall call out for thee. Become necessary unto us. With the morning and evening light, at noon and at midnight, may we feel the need of thy companionship. Wherever our hearts open may we be within the sweet influence of thy nature; and though thou dost not speak as man speaks, yet thou canst call out to us; and the soul shall know thy presence, and shall understand by its own self what thou meanest. Grant unto us this witness of the Spirit, this communion of the soul with thee—and not only once or twice: may we abide in the light.

Thou hast come unto thine own; and even as of old, thine own know thee not, and believe thee not. How many are there present to-night that have learned thy name upon their mother's knee, but have forgotten it! How many are there that grew up into the happiness of a childhood in which piety presided, but have gone away, and have not come back again to their first love and to their early faith! How many who have been tossed about in the world have taken their views of experience from this mortal life in its lowest forms! How many are there marching on now in the Sahara of indifference and in the wilderness of unbelief! How many are there without God and without hope in this world! What shall become of them? Shall they perish, as the fruit? Shall they go out, as a light extinguished? Lord, look upon them; and if there be present such, to-night, have merciful thoughts toward them, and issue those gracious influences of power by which what is best in them shall lift itself up and bear witness against that which is worst. May we have that righteousness which is in Christ Jesus imparted unto us all. May the things which are just, and pure, and noble, and high become to us dearer than silver or gold. For what in all the world is worth the royalty of our own souls! What can all these things do for us in the day of tribulation! How many have had the reed on which they leaned break! How many who have laid up treasure in our time have seen it scattered as dust is scattered by the wind! How many there have been that have broken through the plans of their life! How many there have been that have tasted at this and that fountain, and found their thirst not slaked! How many there are who know that this life can not build them up nor enrich them! And though they had the whole possession of it, it would bring not contentment, but care, and even desolation of all that is noblest and best.

May men come into new partnership with thee. May they think of that which is best for them. Out of all the distemperatures of this life, and out of all its temptations and fiery influences, O, may there be some that shall escape, and not be overwhelmed with an everlasting destruction.

We pray that thou wilt enable thy servant to speak plainly and truthfully to the inward understanding of all present. Give to them not only a hearing ear, but a heart willing to do the things that are right. May we become simple as children, not that we may be deceived, but that we may follow out the evident intention of the truth, and fulfill all its rule and law.

Bless us through life; and when at last the sign comes, O, let the gates of pearl be opened, and let us discern what it means to die : that it is to begin life—the ungroaning life—the life without temptation and without sin—the glorious life of the soul, set free from the drudgery and bondage of the body!

Closing Prayer.

GRANT unto us, our heavenly Father, the divine light and leading. May we walk in the way of the Lord, striving after all Christian experience and grace.

Thou art our Schoolmaster. May we submit ourselves to thy discipline and teaching; for thou hast called us, and said that we should find rest to our souls. O Lord, look upon these turbulent unillumined hearts. Have compassion upon the weary and heavy laden. Call again, and call those who are in thy presence now, saying, Come unto me, and learn of me, and I will give you rest. And grant, we pray thee, that when life is over, we who have come together in this place, in Christ Jesus, and sung together, and prayed together, and moved iu sweet and true fellowship, rising above the weakness of death and triumphing over mortality, may meet in the kingdom of thy glory, clasping inseparable hands, and giving to the Father, Son, and Spirit immortal praises.

Invocation.

GRANT unto us, not outward thoughts, but the inward movement of thy soul, O our Father. Send to us the angels of peace, of gladness, and of hope. May every one of us, with a clear sky though it be night, illumined with thy coming in the midst of sorrow and trouble, have to-day the promise, through Jesus Christ, our Lord; and may we accept him after the inward man re-created in righteousness. We pray that we may be joined together by true Christian fellowship, in thy sanctuary, which thou hast made very precious to us by our experiences of days gone by—experiences of gladness, or experiences of penitential sorrow bringing forth gladness. In this place, by thine appearing, lead every one to-day to feel that Christ hath come from out of the heaven, and hath been enshrined in his own soul.

The Faithfulness of Christ.

Sunday Evening, March 17, 1875.

WE thank thee, thou blessed Saviour, that thou art made known to us not only by thy words, but by thy work in our own hearts. We bear witness that thou hast come to us according to thy promise. Not alone hast thou come to us in times of trouble, but thou hast entered in to abide, and hast been a constant Guest, unprovoked by sins most provoking, and unwearied by tasks most needless put upon thee. Thou hast carried our sins, thou hast borne our sicknesses, and our trouble has been thine. By the word of thy mouth and by the power of thy Spirit thou hast given us light and joy and inspiration; and by faith and hope we have continued until this time. And we are to continue; for from all the memories of the past, and from the blessedness of experiences not forgotten, we derive hope and courage for the future. Having borne us thus far thou wilt not readily cast us aside. Having known our selfishness, our pride, our vanity, our sordidness, our secular and earthly disposition, our life that is in the flesh, our stumbling, our ignorance, our dullness and our frequent resistance of the blessedness of thy will—having known these things, and borne them long, thou wilt still carry us and still bear with us until thy work is perfected. And O, how great will be the glory of thy love, and the wonder of thy patience, and the beauty of thy whole nature and administration, when thou shalt present us before the throne of thy Father, spotless, without blemish or wrinkle!

We rejoice that our salvation stands in thee, and

not in ourselves. It is not because we are wise, it is not because we are fully purposed to follow the Christian life, it is not because we are conscious that from year to year we are growing toward the spirit and away from the flesh, that we hope to be saved. It is in thee that we trust. By reason of thy faithfulness we have courage to believe that having begun a work in us thou wilt continue that work until the consummation and the victory.

And now, Lord, accept our thanksgiving; and give us the joy, to-night, of thy conscious presence. Speak words of comfort to those that are in trouble. Send light to those that are in darkness. Be consciously near to those who seem to themselves to be alone, and cry out to thee in the solitude of their souls, and wonder that thou dost not hear. But thou, O God, dost hear the faintest cry. None are in trouble that thou dost not know it. Thou wilt avenge thine own elect though thou dost tarry long. Thou wilt bring to pass the blessings of thy grace in every soul that trusts in thee.

Bless all that are present here to-night, whether they are hoping in thee or whether, being without God, they are hoping in this world. We pray that the ears of those who are accustomed to hear the truth may not grow dull; may their hearts not become hard; may the word of truth not lose its germinating power in their life. Bring thou thy Spirit to bear upon their spirits, and bring life out of their death, and health out of their sickness, and strength out of their weakness. May thy righteousness avail with every one, and may every one be willing to be clothed of thee, and not of himself. If there are those who have faintly aspired to live the Christian life, and yet have become discouraged, and gone some way backward, wilt thou not revive thy work in them? If there be those that are bound hand and foot in evil habits against which their whole nature revolts, and against which they cry out—O thou that didst come to open the prison doors, and to break the chain and the shackle, wilt thou not look upon thy captives? And by thy supernal power wilt thou not lift them out of the turmoil of evil, and the stress of temptation, and the invincibleness of habit? We pray for all those that are bound; for all those that are in trouble and cannot find relief; for all those that are conscious of their misery and yet are helpless; for all those that seem to themselves marked and sent forward unto death. Lord, make thyself to appear the redeemer of men. Come, we beseech of thee, to seek and to save the lost. Ransom the captives,

Bring back again to their lost faith those whose eyes and minds have been darkened. Return to the Shepherd and Bishop of their souls those who have wandered far and wide.

We pray that, to-night, the Spirit of God may fill this congregation with its presence. May there be many here whose hearts shall be pricked. May there be many whose souls shall be aroused. May the word of thy truth be efficacious for thine own name's sake, and for thine honor's sake.

We pray for all those throughout our land who are preaching the word of God. May they be strengthened in body and mind. May they be renewed with royal courage. May those who are laboring in new and waste places, and laying foundations in the midst of sickness and weakness and trial, be greatly sustained by the presence of their Lord; may they be convoyed in their work; and may there be raised a generation of men who shall be willing to lay foundations even though other men are to build the superstructure thereon. May there be multitudes of holy men who shall rejoice to go forth and labor among the poor and needy, suffering deprivation themselves, and looking for their reward in the heavenly land.

How fast we are marching thither! How the praise and the honors of men wither like flowers that, being plucked, have no roots! How quickly fade the brightest joys of life! We are going away from this lower realm. It is not substance on which we tread. The air above us and the earth beneath us are but visions. The true reality is out of sight and out of reach. The ear cannot hear it, the eye cannot see it, nor can the hand handle it; but it exists. We are moving silently, day and night, toward that great realm of unrevealed light where God himself dwells. And we pray that as we are drawing near to the hour which shall fix our joy and destiny, we may feel the shadow of thy wing over us. May our souls hear thine arousing voice. May thy truth be made mighty in us.

And now we thank thee for the blessings of the day; for its lessons; for its comforts; for its enlightenment; and we pray that we may thus be carried from Sabbath to Sabbath, as from mountain-top to mountain-top, until the New Jerusalem shall appear, the joy of the whole earth.

Closing Prayer.

BLESS to our use, we beseech of thee, the word of truth, the ministry of the day, the songs of joy we have sung, the mingling of our affections, our fellowship with each other, the hopes which have been incited in us and the purposes that we have formed. Thou God of the Sabbath that hast given us rest to-day, give us strength to-morrow, and every day of the week, to carry out our resolutions to live better lives. Teach us so to dwell in the higher life of the soul that, being pure in heart, we shall see God.

We ask it in the name of the Beloved, to whom, with the Father and the Holy Spirit, shall be eternal praises.

Invocation.

THOU who art greater than the unwearied sun that bears light and heat and life without exhausting its store, we rejoice in thy fullness. Giving doth not impoverish thee, nor doth withholding make thee rich. We thank thee for all thy bounties to the inward man. Vouchsafe to us, we beseech of thee, this day, some portion, that our understanding may be enlightened, that our faith may be inspired, that our hope may be kindled, that our joy may be resplendent, that we may rise up from dullness and doubt, and from death in things spiritual, and come into the bright light and sympathy of thy nature, that, being sons of God, we may partake of the divine attributes.

For Uplifting.

OUR heavenly Father, if we could come to thee only in a pure state; if those only might come who are upright and perfect, the whole world would go groaning and sorrowing without God and without hope. Thou hast cast forth into life the innumerable mass of mankind, that see thee not, and hear thee not. We stand in all the avenues by which we are brought up, and call out for God, and thou art not found therein. The eye sees, and cannot behold thee. The ear hears, and cannot hear thee. The hand is stretched forth, and cannot take hold upon thee. Thou canst not be interpreted to our consciousness through our material senses. While we gather all knowledges, the knowledge of thee must come by thy Spirit. Thou mayest give us an inward and new discerning power by the communication of thine own self through our spirit-nature.

How can we, then, O Lord our God, but wander in darkness without thee? If from thee comes life and the power of life, sight and the power of sight, spirit and the power of spirituality, what can we do but come to thee when our wants press us? We come empty—as we are; we come imperfect—we have not yet learned the art of perfection; and we come selfish—we have not learned how to carry ourselves with the fullness of power so as not to be selfish. We come to thee that we may have insight, foresight, and knowledge of thy nature, and a knowledge of our own higher and better nature. We come to thee for inspiration, that we may seek ourselves in that which is beyond; that we may live away from things gross, animal, earthly, secular, and toward things invisible and eternal.

Grant, we pray thee, this morning, the influence

by which that which is best in us shall rise up to greet thee. May we be able to lay aside our burdens, our sordid cares, all animosities, irritations, fears, troubles of every kind—a swarm of the night. Grant that we may stand, this morning, as children of light. May the glory of thy rising touch our heads and enlighten our eyes, as we stand and gaze upon the Sun of righteousness, and feel the healing which is in his beams. We pray for the forgiveness of our sins. We pray for strength to resist temptation and sorrow. We pray for thy sympathy and compassion upon all our infirmities. We pray for thy heart's healing of our griefs. Deliver us from the thrall of selfishness. Deliver us from undue pride. Deliver us from all things that are not leavened with a true kindness. We pray that thou wilt lift us into such a relation to thee, and interpret to us such an understanding of divine life, that we shall ourselves be conscious of our dignity and of our privileges; that we may not walk as other men, bent and bowed down by every storm that sweeps by, but stand steadfast, immovable, always abounding in the work of the Lord.

We pray, especially, for all who have come up hither conscious of their need. We pray for those to whom home seems desolate and lonesome, and who have sought here some cheer and comfort. May the house of God be better to every one of us than our own homes. May it seem better to us than the familiar threshold of our own residence. May it be the gate of heaven to us.

If there be those who come up hither with hearts torn with troubles and sorrows, may they find here, not only an hour's rest, but that cordial, that hope, that inspiration, that trust in God, that sense of divine providence, that faith in the sympathy of God to them, which shall enable them to take their own trouble again when they go home, more elate and more victorious over it, thus making themselves superior to their circumstances. May we know the divine art of casting our burdens on thee and leaving them there. For how often have we come and released ourselves for the moment, but taken back again upon our shoulders the wearisome load. We beseech of thee that thou wilt send light into the darkness of the household, wherever it is; that thou wilt send joy to those who are without comfort, strength to those who seem ready to perish with weakness, and the sense of divine presence to those who seem abandoned of men; and that thou wilt send cure to those who are heartsick.

We pray that thou wilt be with every one in thy presence, this morning, who comes hither in a spirit of supplication. Let them at least touch the hem of thy garment, and receive healing. Let them meet thine eye in benignity, and know that their case is heard of God.

Bless thou the children of the households that are here represented. We give thanks for those who rejoice in their children. We pray for those, who, heavy-hearted, would pray for their children. We crave wisdom, patience, gentleness, in those that are rearing their young for life and for immortality. If there be children that are wandering, this morning, recall them; bring them back again to the fold. If there be those who have gone far away, and whom the eye cannot see, nor even the thought follow, we pray that, wherever they are, hidden or lost, they may be restored. O thou that goest forth to seek and to save the perishing, may they be found ! Give renewed confidence to those who put their faith and trust in thee. Thy covenants are sure.

Closing Prayer.

GRANT, our Father, thy blessing to rest upon the truths of thy record. Bless us with the inspiration which was vouchsafed to thy people of old. Yield to us the same courage, enthusiasm, and usefulness which characterized them. We pray that thou wilt revive thy work in this church and throughout this community. Grant that men may be more earnest in things that pertain to the invisible kingdom. May they follow God more than they follow men. May they be under the influence of the world to come more than under the influence of the world that now is. And so we beseech of thee that thou wilt raise up in our midst testifying, courageous souls, not that defy human reason, but that stand by the higher reason of God in the midst of human things. Thus honor thyself, glorify thy name, and make thy cause to prosper among men.

Invocation.

THOU hast drawn us to thyself, our Father, by those inward invitations which thy people know; and we thank thee that, by the light of the morning, by the memories of days like this, by the rising up within us of our own conscious wants, by the fragrance of love begun toward thee, by all those emotions and signs which indicate thy presence, thou art calling us. And here we are, standing before thee, and waiting for that blessing which waits for us. Give forth to us divine life. O Spirit of wisdom and of goodness, enlighten our understanding and inflame our hearts, that we may this morning, and in all this day, rejoice before thee in sweet and blessed communion.

The Privileges of Prayer.

THOU hast called us to thyself, most merciful Father, with love and with promises abundant; and we are witnesses that it is not in vain that we draw near to thee. We bear witness to thy faithfulness. Thy promises are Yea and Amen. Thy blessings are exceeding abundantly more than we know or think. We thank thee for the privilege of prayer, and for thine answers to prayer; and we rejoice that thou dost not answer according to our petitions. We are blind, and are constantly seeking things which are not best for us. If thou didst grant all our desires according to our requests, we should be ruined. In dealing with our little children we give them, not the things which they ask for, but the things which we judge to be best for them; and thou, our Father, art by thy providence overruling our ignorance and our headlong mistakes, and art doing for us, not so much the things that we request of thee as the things that we should ask; and we are, day by day, saved from peril and from ruin by thy better knowledge and by thy careful love.

We thank thee, also, that thou dost give to us the things which we ask aright. We thank thee that when we ask right things according to thy will thou art full of bounty, even as the sun is of light, and pourest forth thy gifts freely, and without measure—yea, dost overfill us so that there is not room enough for the blessings thou dost grant unto us. Thy thoughts are full of immeasurable tenderness toward us. Thy purposes concerning us far outrun any conception that we have in ourselves; but the unknown, the infinite, we cannot hope to comprehend in this life. That we are to be redeemed from the power of sin; that we are yet to overcome that which is of the earth, earthy; that we are to rise by the communion of love and by the power of faith into a knowledge of higher verities; that we are to stand in the light of celestial glory in the world beyond; and that we are to dwell together in eternal joy with all the saints of every clime—these things we believe; and yet we cannot compass them. They elude our thought, and run quite out of the reach of our feeling. But we rejoice that thou art preparing us according to thy Word for glory and honor and immortality. We pray that we may have in the comfort of these promises day by day an exalted joy over against temptation, over against our frequent stumblings, over against our sins, over against the varied evils which beset us, over against our misfortunes and infirmities, over against the infelicities of our earthly condition, which shall enable us to lift up before our minds the ever-present treasure of thy thoughts and purposes and administration.

Thou hast been, like us, tempted and tried. Thou art the Sufferer. Thou didst lay down thy life for those that suffered, that they might be delivered from suffering. Yea, thou hast suffered that suffering itself might be sanctified, and might be for the good of those that bear it patiently.

And may we be willing to take thy chastisements. May we not find fault with thy dealings with us. Though we feel thy rod at times; though trouble is burdensome to us, and though we are sometimes tempted to complain, to feel that the earth hath forsaken us, that Providence hath forgotten us, and that mischief alone pursues us, yet grant that out of these doubting and rebellious thoughts against thy love we may be lifted up, may feel that the Lord doeth right, and may believe that the tendency of things shall by and by be made plain to us, and that we may learn patience from them. May we learn endurance, may we learn courage, and may we rejoice that we are accounted worthy to suffer. May we learn that the Lord lays no heavier burden upon us than he gives us strength to bear; and so may we be comforted. May we wait patiently upon the Lord, having faith that whatever befalls us is for our welfare; that he will come in his own time and in his own way, and that we shall be delivered; that our feet shall stand upon a rock, and that we shall lift up a voice of rejoicing.

We pray for all those who are tried in spirit; for all those who are in a necessitous condition; for all those who are perplexed, and know not which way to turn; for all those who are in ignorance; for all those who are under peculiar temptations; for all those whose hearts are wrung with anxious thoughts which they cannot express; for all those who feel that they are alone, who seem to themselves to have no guidance, and who are strangers in a strange land. To whom can they turn but unto thee? O may they turn unto thee and take thee by the hand! And wilt thou be their Leader and their Guide, rescuing them from evil and from temptation, giving them power over whatever is wrong, and bringing them into a large place, and establishing their goings.

Wilt thou bless the young that are in our midst. We pray that they may be preserved from snares and pitfalls. May they grow to a nobler manhood than ours. May they advance beyond the line which their fathers reach. With growing opportunity may there be growing endeavor and attainment.

We pray for the peace of Zion. We pray that all roots of bitterness may be taken away; that all disagreement may cease; that all bickerings and envyings and jealousies and hatreds among the people of God may disappear. Roll them down into eternal night, and let them be destroyed for evermore! We pray that unity and co-operation and courage in things good may prevail all over our land, and throughout the whole world. Let thy kingdom come and thy will be done, on earth as it is in heaven.

We ask it in the adorable name of Jesus, to whom, with the Father and the Holy Spirit, shall be praises evermore. *Amen.*

Closing Prayer.

OUR Father, we beseech of thee, accept the offerings that we bring to thee of devotion, of sweet communion in prayer, of praises and aspirations in song. May the recital of our joys and yearnings and desires be acceptable to thee. Give to us, not according to the wisdom of our asking, but according to thine everlasting wisdom. Do for us that which we need, though it bring crying with it. Chasten us, so testifying that thou dost love us, and at the last take us to thyself. And to thy name shall be the praise forever and ever.

www.ingramcontent.com/pod-product-compliance
Lightning Source LLC
Chambersburg PA
CBHW031817220426